MW01531317

Suitcase
Carrier
for
God

Nancy Gayle Cobb

PUBLISH AMERICA

PublishAmerica
Baltimore

First printing

ISBN: 1-4241-9398-2
PUBLISHED BY PUBLISHAMERICA, LLLP
www.publishamerica.com
Baltimore

Printed in the United States of America

Suitcase Carrier for God

Nancy Gayle Cobb

Copywritten Material

* * *

Every attempt has been made to contact every living person in this
book. Except for some names who have been changed to protect their
privacy, everything actually happened as written. This is a true story.

Psalm 96:3[1]
"Publish His glorious deeds among the nations.
Tell everyone about the amazing things He does."

Psalm 78:4, 5b, 6, 7[2]
"We will not hide these truths from our children
but tell the next generation about the glorious
deeds of the Lord. We will tell of his power
and the mighty miracles he did.
He commanded our ancestors to teach them
to their children, so the next generation might
know them—even the children not yet born—
that they—in turn might teach their children.
So each generation can set its hope anew
on God, remembering his glorious
miracles and obeying his commands."

Acknowledgments

My deepest appreciation to those who edited or helped with this project: Dan Boling, Ph. D (deceased), Susan Duke, Pam High, Ann Knox, Della Rentfrow (deceased), Sid Rich, Christie Schroeter, Rev. Jim Walters

Special thanks to Ann Knox for designing the front cover artwork.

My loving husband of 50 years, Joe—Thank you for your prayers while I was on the mission field and for being willing to go it alone while I was gone. Thank you for your support and blessing, for without them there would have been no trips. And thank you for your many hours of critiquing my manuscript and for your wisdom with words. I couldn't have written this book without you!

Our three beautiful trophy daughters, Cyndi Scott, Cathi Page, and Cami Conrad—Thank you for being just as beautiful on the inside as you are on the outside. Thank you for loving me, encouraging me and supporting my mission trips.

Our sons-in-law, Bob Scott, Gary Page and Dr. Curt Conrad, whose lives are a tribute to God. Thank you, too, for your prayers, support and guidance for my trips.

Our ten blue-ribbon grandchildren—Misti, Crystal, Preston, Parker, Don, Joel, Seth, Cristen, Cassie, Cathleen—and our new grandson-in-law, Mike—Thank you for your prayers and support. My prayer for you is that you will be radical for Jesus in whatever call God has on your lives.

My Lord Jesus Christ, the author of each life experience in every chapter of this book. Thank you for allowing me to endure these trials that I might learn to trust You and see your loving faithfulness to your many promises in your blessed Word. To you goes all the glory, honor and praise for making this book possible. I love you.

Dedication

To Joe

my loving and faithful husband, spiritual leader, sweetheart,
my best friend, and the most godly man I know.

Foreword

In The sixth chapter of Isaiah, he said, "I saw the Lord seated on a throne, high and exalted." The presence of the Lord brought conviction to his heart. He heard the Lord say, "Whom shall I sent, and who will go for us?" Isaiah then said, "Here am I; send me."

Hundreds of people have prayed this same prayer. They have said, "Send me." What a privilege to be asked of the Lord to go into all the world and share the good news of Jesus. A large part of the world does not know Jesus. They are waiting for some one to come.

This exciting book takes you to the mission field in many parts of the world. You will be blessed as you follow her in the wonderful things she has seen God do. She is very careful to give Jesus all the praise and glory.

I have served with Nancy Cobb on the mission field. The people loved her for her love for Jesus and for them. You will see through her eyes how God is moving around to save souls.

Nancy hopes this book will encourage others to catch the vision of this great work. I recommend the reading of this book. It gives a clear picture of the work of volunteers on mission fields.

I count it a privilege and honor to write this forward.

Calvin Beach
Former President of International Crusades
(Commissions)

Contents

Preface

Why missions? Why me? I suspect my deceased grandmother, Nelia Stockman Hall, whom we affectionately called Mam-maw, had something to do with it. Mam-maw was my hero. She was the epitome of everything right and good, and, oh, how she loved Jesus.

Every Sunday morning on the way to our little country church, my sister, brother and I would beseech her to tell us the Jesus story. And she was always anxious to oblige.

From my early years I wanted to live my life for God. I'm sure Mammaw's prayers and her walk with God influenced me before I was old enough to remember it. No doubt I was told that Jesus loves me since I was in the bassinet.

Unfortunately, I don't remember when I received Jesus as my Lord and Savior. I was very young and don't remember a time when I didn't want to serve God with all my heart. I wanted to join the church while my dad, a U.S. Army career man, was stationed in Germany during World War II. We went to Walnut Creek Baptist Church, the suburbs of Austin, Texas. My dad's family was Lutheran. Mom was afraid Daddy's family might think she was forcing me into the Baptist church if I joined while he was away, so she asked me to wait until Daddy came home before I joined the church. I was 11 years old when Daddy returned from the war, and he, my brother Tommy, and I all professed Jesus as our Savior and joined the church together.

When I heard stories of missionaries or heard a missionary speak, I thought that was what I wanted to be, because I didn't know any other way to serve God with all my heart. Back then, few churches had secretaries, and in my denomination women were not allowed to preach. The only way I thought I could serve God wholly was to be a missionary. This pleased Mam-maw no end. Undoubtedly, it probably was her idea to start with.

In my elementary-age years I attended GA's (Girls Auxiliary), a mission organization at church. There we studied about missionaries and prayed for them on their birthdays.

During my junior high school years we lived in Eta Jima, an island off Honshu, Japan, where Daddy was stationed. One Sunday my family visited a Baptist mission at Kure, on the mainland. The missionary, Rev. (now Dr.) Curtis Askew, said that our visit did more for his Japanese congregation than a month of his preaching, because they saw that Americans really cared about them. A special memory is when the Japanese sang *What A Friend We Have in Jesus*[3] and my family sang along in English. Fascinated, the congregation snickered and smiled at us as we sang. We were of different cultures and language, but we were all of one spirit and we all recognized that.

Mom invited Rev. Askew to our home to preach to the army wives' hired help which the army provided. Mom talked with our neighbors, army dependent wives, and asked them to allow their hired help to come to our home for Rev. Askew's visits.

The first time he came, Mom let me skip school to stay home for the meeting. I was mesmerized by Rev. Askew's little portable organ that he brought to play while he led the maids, "houseboys," and gardeners in singing the hymns of faith. Of course, he preached in Japanese, which I didn't understand, but after his sermon when men and women raised their hands to indicate they wanted to pray to receive Christ as their Savior, I rejoiced. What an opportunity to witness my first glimpse of mission work on foreign soil. Although I was only 14, I wanted this to be a part of my life.

Back in Texas at my home church, a woman who died had requested that instead of flowers for her funeral, she wanted donations to be given to purchase Japanese printed Bibles to send to us to give to the Japanese people.

Shamasan, our Japanese housemaid, lived on the mainland and traveled back and forth daily across the bay. When the weather was inclement, Shamasan would spend the night with us and sleep in the utility room. How well I remember the night she stayed over after Rev. Askew's first visit. As I passed by the opened door to the utility room, there she sat on her bed reading the little Japanese Bible, her first time ever to read a Bible. She was awed at what she read and trusted Jesus with her life. What a blessing for me, as a young girl, to see a life changed because of our involvement in missions. I am grateful for a mom and dad who gave me that opportunity.

In college I worked in neighborhood missions on a weekly basis where I taught Bible stories and songs, and we played games. It was always a highlight in my week and soon missions got into my blood. From junior high on I thought I would marry a preacher or a missionary, but the closest thing I got to that was marrying a preacher's son. I believe, however, that that was God's will for me and that whether I was at home or on the mission field, I would serve God.

After I married, I joined the WMU (Women's Missionary Union) at church, where we not only studied about missionaries and prayed for them but did community work to help others. Missions had become a natural and regular part of my life, but I still yearned to go to foreign soil to the "mission field."

I "early retired" from teaching school to raise our daughters, but I wanted to do something part-time, so I became a Mary Kay beauty consultant and then a director. For six years in Mary Kay, Inc., unbeknownst to me, God was preparing me for the mission field. Speaking to strangers and talking to groups, large or small, became easy for me. Eventually I would see how God had used jobs and opportunities in my life to prepare me for the future.

Learning to deal with people in Mary Kay had certainly been a big part in preparing me for the mission field and erasing any fear I might have in talking to strangers. And living in Germany and Japan with an army dad took away any fear I might have in traveling to foreign countries. Little did I know how God was setting me up to fulfill my childhood dream.

One day I was invited to hear Barbara Arbo at a women's retreat. At the end of the teaching, Barbara asked for all women who especially felt a call of God on their lives to raise their hands. I shot up my hand. She then asked those women to come forward to receive a special word from God.

Thrilled, I hurried forward and nervously awaited my turn. Mrs. Arbo placed her hand on my head, paused for a moment, and then spoke.

"A different segment of people. A different segment of people," she said.

That was it. That was all? What did it mean? I didn't know what it meant and neither did Barbara, but that's what she believed she received from the Lord. Since I had been working on writing a book, I assumed that possibly it meant my book would be published and read by people all over the United States—different segments of people.

A few months, later, however, I made my first mission trip, to South America, and I knew then that my mission trip was the meaning of the words Mrs. Arbo had received from God.

More than anything, I contribute my desire for missions to the prayers of my precious Mam-maw. She was a prayer warrior, and as I stood on foreign soil time after time, sharing the love of God and His salvation, I knew that Mam-maw was there with me, in spirit, cheering me on.

Colombia, 1983

1

"Go Ye into All the World..."

"On the last crusade we averaged 50 decisions for Christ for each team member," Brenda McWhorter (Massingill) enthusiastically shared at my church one Sunday morning. A teenager with larger-than-life, dancing black eyes, she reflected love and excitement for International Crusades, a Southern Baptist organization. This was no ordinary mission program, I surmised. Fifty salvations in one week per team member was one whale of a ministry. Could it possibly mean if I went on a crusade 50 people would be born again in a single week? That's what it sounded like. If a teenager could do it, surely this schoolteacher could. Deep within I had a longing to win souls for Jesus, so I listened further.

"Language is no barrier," Brenda said. Picking up a cardboard contraption she called a disco, she unfolded it, placed a phonograph record on it and played it by turning the record with a pencil. I couldn't understand the words. Then she said the message was the plan of salvation in Spanish. "Each team member has a disco as well as his own printed personal testimony translated into Spanish," she went on to say. "On one page of the testimony sheet is a list of questions in Spanish to help lead the lost to Christ. On the opposite page is the same list of questions in English so we can follow along and know what the Colombian is reading. Language is definitely no barrier here.

"A church member accompanies the team member in visitation, introduces him to the nationals and helps if there are questions from the nationals," Brenda related.

The next trip, to Bogota, Colombia, was in six months. International Crusades (IC), only ten years old, was new to me. Seven Southern Baptist laymen who wanted to spread Jesus' message to the world birthed the organization.

I was excited and wanted my husband and me to go. He didn't feel God leading him on the mission but agreed to go with me to the initial meeting to learn more about it. After the meeting I was even more convinced God wanted me to go. Joe, however, still felt God was not leading him in that direction. We decided that instead of making a decision right then we would continue to pray about it.

We had always worked together in church activities, and I assumed if the Lord didn't lead Joe to go, then I wasn't to go either. Weeks passed and every day I felt God was calling me to Bogota, but Joe was assured He was not calling him.

We discussed the trip on the way to church one morning when Joe said, "Honey, if you think you're supposed to go, then go! Don't let me keep you from going." I needed to hear those words. They released me to go, and I was so thankful for a husband who gave me the freedom to do what I thought was God's will.

That morning our Sunday school lesson was from Isaiah. As I flipped through the Bible my eyes fell on the underlined scripture, "How lovely ON THE MOUNTAINS are the feet of him who brings good news, who announces peace, and brings good news of happiness, WHO ANNOUNCES SALVATION."[4] Bogota was in the Andes Mountains. When I saw the words "on the mountains" it was like hearing a gigantic brassy clanging in my brain. God was speaking . I sighed deeply as my eyes filled with tears; indeed, I was going to Bogota. I was so stunned by God's intervention, that I blurted my good news out in class. I could hardly wait to tell Joe.

As soon as Sunday school was over I searched him out to tell him how God had confirmed I was to be on the team to Bogota. His eyes filled with such love and joy that once more I knew God was confirming that my decision to go was His will.

Fifty souls would be my goal. Cyndi, our oldest daughter, told me, "Mom, I'm going to pray you'll win double your goal to the Lord." Her challenge humbled me. Just 50 sounded pretty good to me. My first mission trip was underway.

I was enthusiastic about going, but I still believed Joe would be led to Bogota, too. When he didn't, my enthusiasm subsided, as I didn't want to go without him.

Two months before departure I realized I couldn't go on a mission trip with a discouraged attitude. Frankly, I didn't care about Colombians. I wanted to care about them, but I simply didn't have a burden for them. All I could think about was what clothes to pack, what gifts to take, and whether we would we get to see Miami Beach on our layover. I busied myself preparing for the trip, but my heart wasn't in it.

I knew I needed a change of attitude, so I asked LaDonna Thurman to be my prayer partner for the trip, as we had prayed together weekly for years. We prayed for the Colombians, those preparing for the crusade, financial aid for team members, and especially lost souls. We prayed God would give me a burden for the Colombians and that He would fill me with love for those people.

By our last prayer meeting prior to the trip, God had, indeed, answered every prayer. We made no more requests of God. Instead, that last prayer meeting we only offered up praise for all He had done to prepare me for this crusade. My attitude had done an about-face. I was so grateful for a God who not only called me to Bogota but who also prepared my heart for the trip.

While packing my suitcases I could hardly wait for my first mission trip to begin. I was going to be a suitcase carrier for God.

2

The Vision of Flying Guardian Angels

My first mission trip was a long way from home, but I told family members, "The safest place in the world is in God's will." Now that I had boarded the jetliner, however, I was nervous at the prospect of flying into an unknown situation.

Although I was excited about witnessing to the Colombians, thoughts of my husband, my three daughters, and my grandchildren closed in on me. Mixed emotions seemed to be the order of the hour. I leaned back in the seat, closed my eyes and listened to my heart thumping fervently as the plane lifted off.

Thy will be done, was my heart's cry.

Then I thought of the 94 mission team members on the airplane and of the guardian angels assigned to each of us. What a great host of angels that would be.

Suddenly, a picture came into my mind. Some, perhaps, might call it a vision. Our guardian angels were lined up beneath the jet, from wingtip to wingtip and from the nose to the tail, pushing the plane onward. Their long, white robes billowed about them as they pushed the plane forward.

Then it was as if I was below the airplane, looking up. I gasped at the beauty of it: a huge white cross moving through the sky. *How symbolic,* I thought, *since we're taking the good news of Jesus Christ to Bogota.*

After meditating on my vision for a moment and thanking God for His reassurance of protection, I opened my Bible to the day's appointed readings. "Protect me, O God. I trust in you for safety...my future is in your hands…and so I am thankful and glad, and I feel completely secure, because you protect me from the power of death…and you will not abandon me to the world of the dead. You will show me the path that leads to life."[5]

Amazed at the timing of this scripture, I smiled at God's reassurance. He knew I would need that verse on this very day. I closed my Bible and relaxed into the seat. Anxiety was gone. God, in His loving way, had given me victory over fear. He was my Protector whether I was at home, on foreign soil or in the air, and peace was mine.

3

Rewards of Uncompromising Faith

One of my favorite parts of a mission trip was meeting and getting to know team members who had uncompromising faith. Myron Coates, a fiery young man from my church, was short $500 for his ticket the day we left for Bogota. He was so sure he was meant to go that he packed and met our team at the airport two hours before takeoff, in spite of his lacking finances.

We stood around, marveling at Myron's faith, yet wondering if he might be a bit addled, coming to the airport without a ticket. We prayed that somehow, someway, God would provide a last-minute miracle.

Moments before boarding I saw Myron hugging a man who had just arrived. I thought maybe he was part of our team, but I soon learned he was a friend of Myron's. He had driven all night from Dallas to Oklahoma and back to get a $500 check, contributed from a friend for Myron, because he knew Myron needed it. Myron knew nothing of the trip. Need it, indeed!

Myron's faith had held him up, and it was my first experience at seeing God fulfill financial needs for mission trips.

Kelly and Ellen Adkins also have a story of uncompromising faith. They believed God had called them to go on a mission trip to Brazil, yet they didn't have the finances for it. Kelly was a student at Southwestern Baptist Theological Seminary, and times were hard, but he and Ellen were convinced they were meant to go.

They sent for their visas, Kelly prepared all his sermons and Ellen packed three suitcases of clothing and gifts for the churches.

Kelly called Ben Mieth, then president of International Crusades, to see if he could come to the airport even though he didn't have a ticket. Ben said, "Yes," but told him that IC didn't have any money that they could help him with.

The day of departure arrived and only $305 for each of their tickets had come in. They were $2,600 short of the funds needed. They took their suitcases to the church, and it was there that Ellen decided she wouldn't plan to go this time, but she continued to pray for Kelly's financial miracle on the bus to the airport with the team.

As team members arrived from other churches and checked in their baggage, Kelly and Ellen stood by watching and waiting for their miracle. Finally, Ben and Dr. Tom Robuck, the Adkins' pastor, came over to talk to Kelly.

Ben said, "I called everyone I could think of and there are just no more funds available."

"You know, you took a step of faith, and that is important," Dr. Robuck encouraged.

Smiling, Kelly responded, "Brother Tom, it is not time to give up yet. We have five minutes left before the plane leaves."

Brother Tom then went to join the others boarding the plane. Because everyone had left the waiting area to board the plane, the Adkins were the only ones left in the waiting area. They sat on Kelly's suitcases and prayed.

When the team coordinator, John Hoogendorn, learned of the Adkins' situation and that they apparently wouldn't be getting on the plane, he approached Dr. Bill Elliff, who was leading a team from his church on the trip.

"There is a couple from Ft. Worth who were not able to get the money for their tickets and will not be able to come on the crusade. Can you and your team pray for them before you get on the plane?" John asked.

"How much do you need?" Dr. Elliff asked.

"Two thousand six hundred dollars," John answered, never dreaming of the words Dr. Elliff would say next.

"Tell them to get on the plane. I have the money right here," Dr. Elliff responded, patting his hip pocket. The amount he had with him wasn't just close. It was, to the dollar, the exact amount they needed, as if God Himself was saying, "Let there be no doubt who is the author of this miracle." As it turned out, the previous Wednesday night at Dr. Elliff's church the mission team had been short several thousand dollars for the trip, so at the close of his sermon, he mentioned to his congregation of the need. After the service people began to put checks and bills in his pocket. When he went to his office and pulled it all out, there was enough to cover everyone's trip including extra money. Since he didn't know who had donated it all, he didn't know how to return it and decided he'd figure it out after he returned from the mission trip.

Kelly looked up from his praying. He stood up and was about to go over to the American Airlines ticket counter to say, "We really believe that it is God's will for us to go on this mission. Is there anyone here who can grant us permission to make the trip, even without tickets?"

Suddenly Kelly looked up to see Brother Tom come running around the corner with tears streaming down his cheeks. Kelly hurried to meet him, thinking that someone on their team had become ill or, perhaps, had collapsed or died.

"Brother Tom, what's the matter?" Kelly asked.

"I don't understand all of this yet, but your way has been paid to Brazil. Get your bags and get on the plane," Brother Tom expounded.

"Me?" Kelly asked.

"No. You and Ellen both!"

The team went wild on the plane, rejoicing and shouting praises to God, and "high-fiving" one another as Kelly and Ellen boarded the jetliner. Ellen, strangely enough, had her passport and visa in her purse, because she had put them there earlier in the week, still hoping for a financial miracle. She hadn't even remembered they were in her purse. She boarded the plane with nothing but the clothes on her back and her purse. With help from team members she was able to borrow clothes and other necessities to supply her every need for the two-week trip.

Yes, one of the highlights of my trips was hearing stories of people with uncompromising faith like Myron, Kelly and Ellen. I was beginning to learn that what God begins, He definitely finishes.

4

My Special Pink Church

Arriving at Bogota proved to be an humbling experience. Outside of the airport's glass walls, throngs of nationals waved and stretched to see us, still inside the airport.

As we came through the sliding doors, tear-stained brown faces met us with smiles, welcoming us to their country. One young man, probably in his early 20s, wept with joy as he energetically shook my hand. Something strange happened inside me. I didn't know that man, but I loved him.

Women held their children up to us, and I kissed one little girl. They offered praise to God and thanked us for coming. My heart was already so full I couldn't imagine the trip getting any better. *Oh, God, what if I hadn't come?* I thought.

I was reminded of Jesus and, later, of Paul as they ministered on the streets and how people would try to touch them. Several reached out to touch me. I wanted to cry out, "No, don't! I'm nobody!" My heart broke as these people welcomed us with such love. Mesmerized, I sat quietly on the bus ride to our hotel as I pondered our overwhelming welcome.

"Oh, God. Do something through me this week," I begged.

I had prayed for God to choose my roommate and the church to which I would be assigned. Although I had been scheduled to go to Tunja with my church's team, the week before we left we were reassigned to stay in Bogota.

I roomed with Mary Beyers, who had also visited our church with the IC group. She humorously considered herself a "professional volunteer" and had been on many crusades. She had personally recruited 25 people for this trip. I was honored to be Mary's roommate, because she knew the ropes about mission trips, and I was full of questions.

Mary said that we might visit the town where other teams were, to encourage and help them. Our mission team's coordinator, Jim Walters, considered Mary his "right hand man." She had lists of things to purchase and do. Whatever Jim needed, she did it.

I recognized these activities as important, but running errands wasn't my reason for coming. I wanted to get out there and play my disco. How could I lead people to the Lord without witnessing?

Since the Tunja church had dropped out of the crusade, we were placed on an already full team. Since we had been shifted around, I didn't feel needed, and discouragement set in. I met the pastor, an enthusiastic, joy-filled saint, from our newly assigned church, and my discouragement soon faded.

God let me know He was in control of my situation, as dismal as it seemed. So I told the Lord if He had sent me on this trip to follow Mary around, that's what I'd do. I prayed God would show me exactly what He wanted from me so I would have no doubt. Then God's sense of humor entered the picture.

My favorite color is pink; all shades of pink. On occasion I've been called the "Pink Lady" and some refer to pink as "my color." I walked into Bethany Church ready to do what God required, whatever that was, only to stop dead in my tracks. I had asked God for a sign, and there it was, a 30-foot-high sanctuary with walls painted bright pink. I burst out laughing. God certainly had let me know, in His unique way, that this was where I was supposed to be. I had never seen a pink church before. I knew in my spirit God was speaking loud and clear—THIS was where I belonged. I marveled at God who cared enough to pamper His kid.

Not only had I been dubbed "The Pink Lady" back home, but also "The Flower Lady" by neighborhood kids because of my love for growing flowers. As we drove through the neighborhood of our church,

I noticed the many flowers that I had not seen in other parts of Bogota. The yards were so colorful that I mentioned it to our interpreter, who told me this neighborhood was called El Jardin, which, translated, means The Garden.

Isn't that just like God, I thought, *to set me down right in the smack-dab-middle of a neighborhood called The Garden in a bright pink church. Just another confirmation that I'm exactly where I'm supposed to be. What a loving God I serve!* I marveled that with all the lost souls at stake, my loving Father would take time to quiet my heart. Then I remembered that His precious Word says He's concerned about every detail of my life.

I soon learned to love the pastor, whose personality exhibited a winning sense of humor, but he also wept for people's lost souls. I quickly learned to love his people as well, as their enthusiasm for the Lord blessed me. *What a wonderful place to be*, I thought. *Thank you, Jesus, for my special pink church.*

5

The Joys of Witnessing

I'd never been so all alone as I was in Bogota, yet I knew Jesus was with me, so I never felt for a minute that I was alone. At one time, a hair-raising taxi ride had me reading Psalm 91 (the Protection Psalm) orally to our team. I needed that assurance when our taxi driver almost hit an elderly woman who gave him "what for" as she shook her fist at him.

We arrived at our church and were waiting for some church members to arrive, when we saw four teenagers at a nearby park. A team member decided to share with these young people, so I followed him to the park.

While I played the disco for the teenagers, turning the record with a pencil, another young man walked up to listen. The four teenagers did not receive Christ, but the young man, who, out of curiosity walked up, accepted the Lord as his personal Savior. He came to church that night and made his profession of faith public. He also brought his wife, who committed her life to Christ, too. What a way to start the week!

Another time, as we passed an elderly man on the street I handed a tract to him. I looked back to see if he was reading it, and saw him talking excitedly about the tract to his friend. I realized that at his age it might be his last opportunity to receive Christ so we went back, played the disco, and I shared my testimony. This 80-year-old readily prayed to receive Christ. With tears in his eyes he shook our hands again and again and thanked us over and over. I left with tears flooding my eyes, praising God for His allowing me the opportunity to share His wonderful love and salvation to the people of Bogota. I actually was becoming a missionary, and I loved it.

As I sat in church I remembered being about ten years old when I played the hymn *The Old Rugged Cross* on the piano at church while my grandmother led the congregational singing. I wanted to be a missionary even then, and I thought how happy Mam-maw would be to know her little Nancy Gayle was on the mission field. I knew I was in Colombia because God was still answering her prayers. I hoped that, somehow, she knew I was there, and I knew if she did, she would be smiling.

To get 50 decisions for the Lord, I needed ten each day for the five days we would be witnessing. The Lord convicted me, however, for putting an emphasis on numbers. I asked His forgiveness and told Him that whatever He wanted was fine with me. I'd do the witnessing and leave the increase to Him.

That night before Bible study I counted up my day's work and found that nine had prayed to receive Christ. There was only one woman at the Bible study who was not a believer. During the evening she accepted Christ. That was number ten! *Thank you, Lord*, I prayed. Seeing how He worked through us to grant our desires AFTER we surrendered to His ways was an eye-opener.

We visited one home where I gave my testimony in broken Spanish. I don't know the Spanish verbs well, so I just put together main words I could recall. It had been 30 years since I took one year of college Spanish, and I was amazed that I could put together enough words for a testimony. Mary Beyers told me that God has a way of bringing back to our memory what we need in witnessing. I was convinced, to say the least.

We visited a beauty shop where three Jehovah Witnesses worked. I told Jose, my interpreter, that it was usually difficult to witness to Jehovah Witnesses. Jose had been a believer for two years and served as a pillar in the church. He tried to encourage me by reminding me that God was with us. I knew that, of course, but was still nervous about witnessing to Jehovah Witnesses.

These were friends of Jose's, and he assured me they would be kind. We played the disco and I shared my testimony, but right off the bat,

Julia, the shop's owner, said she didn't believe in the Holy Spirit. They were friendly, however, and were not defensive.

I turned in my Bible to read John 20:21-22[6] to her: "Jesus therefore said to them again, 'Peace be with you, as the Father has sent me, I also send you.' And when He had said this, He breathed on them and said to them, 'Receive the Holy Spirit.'" When I finished, Julia nodded as if to say, "Okay." All three women prayed to receive the Lord. Obviously, the Holy Spirit had already been at work.

Another day as Maria, my church helper, and I walked through the neighborhood, we passed a leper standing with a crutch. I thought of the scripture "But Peter said, 'I do not possess silver and gold, but what I do have I give to you. In the name of Jesus Christ the Nazarene—walk!'"[7] As we walked past him I thought, *How can I not stop?*

We walked on a few feet and I knew I had to go back. I told Maria, *"Aqui"* ("Here" in English) and pointed to the leper. She looked bewildered, and obviously did not want to witness to the leper, but she reluctantly followed me.

I set the disco down on the sidewalk and began playing it. Soon there were 12 pairs of legs around the disco. When I finished playing, we passed out testimonies. Most people left so I read the questions to the leper in Spanish. He then prayed with Maria to receive Christ. I wanted to tell him God could heal him so I had to look up the word for "heal" in Spanish. I felt like I was walking through the book of Acts. We gave him a New Testament and 300 pesos. As we shuffled on down the street I wept. People stared at me, but I didn't care.

While we played the disco for six teenage boys who were drinking beer outside a local shop, I was reminded of the danger. I tried to think of them as someone's sons or brothers—anything to make them seem less dangerous. It helped. Two of the boys wandered off when some girls came up, but four of the boys prayed aloud in that public place to receive Jesus. When I asked to take their picture one boy took off his jacket to hide the empty beer bottles perched on the fence. These "tough guys" had turned into smiling, gracious, little lambs. The change in them was evident immediately.

We walked on and played the disco in a market for a man who had been reading the newspaper. He was not at all interested in our disco, but agreed to let us play it. He looked hard and rough, and before the disco was finished he began reading his paper again. But as we went through the testimony and questions he warmed up to us and later prayed to receive Christ. The change God made in him proved awesome. When we left he was cordial and thanked us again and again for sharing Jesus with him. The Holy Spirit certainly was doing His work.

That week, in answer to my daughter's prayer, God allowed me to pray with 123 people to receive the Lord. I came home flying high and looking forward to my next trip.

From my journal I read, "With boldness as I hunger to share the gospel, it's almost like a fever. At mealtime I don't care if I eat. I just want to keep on sharing. Although my body may need nourishment, my mind and spirit are so caught up in Jesus that there is no hunger. I wish I could just take this feeling back to the States. Eating supper at 9:00 p.m.. is no big deal. I'm usually so tired that the only reason I eat is for strength for tomorrow."

Missions were in my blood, and life would never be the same.

Peru, 1984

6

Hurry up and Wait

As the plane rolled onto the runway, I turned my head away from the stranger sitting next to me so she couldn't see my tears. Quietly I repeated to myself one last time the words that had become my motto for the past two weeks, "I WILL be on that plane," and now I was. The other side of victory felt fantastic.

Six months earlier I was impressed that I was to go to Peru in June with International Crusades. Joe was unable to finance this trip as he had my first mission trip, so from the beginning we knew God would have to provide.

I knew the only question was whether or not God wanted me to go. If He did, then I believed He would provide. In my spirit, I believed the trip would, somehow, be spectacularly financed. Going on this trip had not been my idea, but God's, as He had broken my heart for the lost world. It had become the most important thing in my life.

In my home cell group, someone said, "He'll provide in a way you won't expect." Those words came back to me time and again.

In January I began to pray scriptures daily. I prayed Philippians 4:19[8], "And my God will liberally supply and fill to the full my every need according to His riches in glory."[2]

EVERY need! LIBERALLY supply! HIS RICHES IN GLORY! What a promise!

Why should I worry? But I did. I hoped to be on that plane, but deep down I wasn't sure that God would actually pay my way. The price of $1,480 was a lot in man's eyes, but it was nothing to God. I was a "man," however, and looked at it from "man's" point of view.

Several months before flight date I asked the Lord to confirm every day, until we were to leave, that I would be on that plane for Peru if He wanted me to go. One morning as I was reading from Joshua, the words "I, myself will send you" jumped off the page at me. My heart pounded, and I knew God was speaking. My big question now was "How?" I wrote the confirmations down each day in my Bible. Once while I was praying about Peru, the Lord spoke to me, "Freely ye have received. Freely give." I knew He meant my life, that I was to go and share the gospel. After a month of confirmations I decided to let Him off the hook. I prayed, "Okay, Lord, I believe you. I AM going to Peru."

Doubts assailed once more as the departure date drew near. Maybe I'd made up those confirmations. They'd come mostly from scripture but also from sermons, songs, even TV. I was bewildered.

One Sunday morning in church a young man told of his recent trip to South America. He wept as he spoke of street children who had no homes and of the immense crime. His experience sounded like my trip to Colombia. My heart began to break once more for the Spanish-speaking people. My whole being cried out to God for these people. I knew that morning that I had to go to Peru. Could I do anything less?

My hopes were high as I told everyone I was going to Peru, even though I still had no money for the trip. What I needed was for my "hope" to change to "faith." I was telling it, but I wavered back and forth trying to believe it. I knew "hope" wouldn't get me on that plane, so I prayed for faith.

Two weeks before flight date my pastor, Dr. Larry Lea, preached, "God will not abandon you. He's promised not to forsake you." I could see myself at the airport with my luggage while the jetliner took off without me. To me that would be abandonment. Surely God would not allow that if He told me to go to Peru. Someone said, "Where God guides, He provides." I planted my faith squarely on that and Philippians 4:19, that God would provide my needs.

I found scripture after scripture that showed God's care and faithfulness, such as "Take delight in the Lord, and He will give you your heart's desire."[9]

Before leaving church that Sunday morning I KNEW I'd be on that plane to Peru. I confessed it to everyone—and I meant it. I didn't have just "hope" anymore; I truly believed it. Even my faith was a gift from God.

Two weeks to go and I'd been so concerned over finances that I'd not even asked anyone to be my prayer partner. For several months before going to Colombia, LaDonna and I prayed weekly for the trip. I had begun walking and jogging every day, and had given up caffeine and carbonated drinks. This physical body had to be in top shape for the mission field. I had prayed and fasted many times for my Colombia trip, for those who would surrender their lives to God.

Now here I was with only two weeks left before traveling to Peru. I had little time to pray or get into shape. It seemed God would have to use me in spite of myself. All I had to offer was to be a willing vessel. I prayed that being unprepared wouldn't keep someone from turning to Christ.

Twelve days before liftoff I couldn't find my passport. It was packed in one of 100 boxes we had stored in three places, but I certainly didn't know where. We were "camping" in part of our unfinished house we were building. I went to every location twice looking for my passport. In a panic I called Jim Walters of IC. He said we could hire a courier to walk it in at Houston, but it would cost $60. *What a waste*, I thought. We had to find that passport!

"Father," I prayed, "You know where that passport is. Please, lead us to it, and if we find it, that will be my one last confirmation that I'll be on that plane to Peru."

Several hours later Joe called with the news that he'd found the passport in an unmarked box in my IC carry-on bag from my Colombian trip. I hooted and hollered and praised the Lord, and danced around, laughing at the devil. Only the Lord could've located that passport in one of 100 boxes. And He had brought it right to us. What a miracle!

Three days before departure, still with no money, I asked our church's staff evangelist, Dr. David Shibley, to pray for me, because I wanted to be sent out by my church. When he laid his hands on me and began to pray, I fell backwards under the power of God and sat right down into an oversized flowerpot of silk flowers. My backside fit perfectly, so perfectly, in fact, that I couldn't get up. There I sat in my choir robe, crying my eyes out; weak under the power of God and I couldn't do anything about it. I couldn't help but wonder if I wasn't quite the sight. Fortunately, my choir robe fell around the flowerpot, so it wasn't as obvious to the congregation what had happened. Finally I was able to pull myself out and went back to my seat.

I decided that if the devil wanted a fight he was going to get one. I began a fast and determined not to eat until the money was accounted for. I called many friends and family to ask for prayer, and packed my bags.

Wednesday, the day of liftoff, arrived. I awoke at 3:45 a.m. and prayed for an hour. While in prayer the Lord spoke to my spirit, "Trust Me." Even though the money wasn't in, the battle was over. It was just a matter of time.

At 9:00 a.m. I called IC. Juanez Beach answered the phone.

"Hi, Juanez. This is Nancy Cobb. You got any miracles for me yet?" I asked.

"No, not yet. Time is getting close," she answered. The wait was on with six hours until liftoff.

About 10:30 the phone rang. Would this be my long-awaited moment?

"Nancy, how are things going?" Jim Walters of IC asked.

"Just great, Jim. What do you know?" I answered, hoping he had some good news for me.

"Nancy, my father-in-law (Bob Brown) is unable to make the trip, and you can go in his place."

"Praise God!" I shouted. I was amazed that I was so at peace. Ordinarily I would have jumped up and down and screamed my lungs out, like when Joe had found the passport. But there was a quietness, a peace, in my spirit. I was convinced the finances would come, and now they had.

Jim said Mr. Brown's co-worker had broken his leg, so Mr. Brown had to stay and run the business. *I got to go on this trip because of a broken leg?* I thought. Would my family give me a hard time about this one! All along God knew it was going to happen.

I thanked Jim and after I hung up the phone I laughed and laughed at God's timing and sense of humor. Then I praised God, thanking Him for His faithfulness.

No, God had not abandoned me. He had not forsaken me. He had liberally supplied my need and had given me my heart's desires. He had answered our prayers, and right on time. Walking with the Lord proved to be anything but dull.

7

Discovering the Trials of Full-Time Missionaries

I was beginning to learn the ups and downs of full-time missionaries. After a fantastic day of 13 decisions for Christ in Trujillo, my interpreter, Gabriel, and I went to a church member's home for snacks. One of his neighbors, Elsie, from Hungary and her daughters, ages seven and nine, were visiting. She and her husband had been in Peru for four years, and although she could speak no English, her daughters could.

After snacks I played the disco for Elsie and her daughters while Gabriel began to read through the questions with them. When he got to the first question, *Do you believe in God?* Elsie shook her head no. Gabriel informed me that Elsie was a Communist and did not believe in God, but she did not object to her nine-year-old praying to receive Christ.

I showed Elsie scriptures that Jesus was the "one mediator" and "one way." She did not argue but did not respond, either. I could hardly believe I was sitting here with a live Communist and loving her because she was so nice. Mostly, though, I knew God was loving her through me. Loving people came easily this week. Elsie was gentle and not at all like I had pictured a Communist. I thought of the scripture that Satan comes in sheep's clothing. I fought back tears and felt helpless as I tried to tell this woman Jesus died for her. My insides wanted to cry out to her, and I felt bound because she wouldn't receive my help. Gabriel tried, but Elsie would not respond. "Her country didn't believe in God," Gabriel told me. It would have been easier had Elsie gotten mad and left. I took her picture as a reminder to pray for her.

When we parted I said, "One last thing, Jesus Christ loves you very much and so do I." Gabriel interpreted it for me, and Elsie smiled, nodding her head in agreement.

My first personal encounter with a Communist was
not a sword, but a smile;
not a uniform, but a mother's dress;
not words of fury, but words of kindness;
not hate, but gentleness;
not terror and fear, but friendship;
not prison walls, but a meal together;
a closed mind on her part, but a broken heart on mine.

I realized the Holy Spirit had to do the drawing and revealing, but it didn't help my pain for Elsie. I realized I needed to pray more, much more. I was beginning to see the difficulties that full-time missionaries had in dealing with Communists.

Another unexpected turn came when I was the only team member at our host church for several days. Sherra and Hayward Armstrong, our host missionaries, had been kind enough to taxi us all week, prepare meals for our team, and couldn't have been more gracious, but I got lonely and homesick and invited myself to a pity party. I was having difficulties with the culture which didn't help my "downys." Before the trip we were told to take dark clothes, but in my closet hung mostly bright-colored clothes. I took a black dress and wore it three days in a row. Finally, the third night Sherra kindly whispered to me that wearing black in Peru meant one was in mourning. I was so embarrassed but so appreciative to Sherra for cluing me in. Then as I was giving my testimony to the church, I wanted to tell the congregation what a fine person their pastor was, and the interpreter whispered to me that the word I had used to describe their pastor had "sexual innuendoes" in Spanish, and did I really want to use that word? Again, I was terribly humiliated and wondered if the Armstrongs had such difficulties learning to live in that culture. I wanted so much to be a good example as a "missionary," but so far I felt I was batting zero. I prayed that God would show me what He wanted me to learn from all of this.

On the way to the mission the next morning I asked Sherra if they had experienced culture shock when they came to Peru.

"Every day," she answered. "You don't get used to it quickly."

Although this was their second term serving on the mission field, Hayward's father and Sherra's brother had died during their furlough. Serving this second term was very difficult for them since there had been some uncertainty of their returning to Peru.

Sherra said they were the only North Americans in the city during their first term and were the first missionaries to come there in ten years. They had not been welcomed by the Peruvians in the beginning, and felt very alone.

As Sherra bared her soul to me I was saddened. I had thought maybe God was trying to help me see how missionaries feel all the time. I had been right, and again, knew I needed to pray constantly for these missionaries who felt so all alone all the time. God had opened my eyes to the trials of being a full-time missionary by allowing me to experience some of their loneliness during their first tour.

When I began to focus on the missionaries' trials, my pity party petered out. Yes, I was lonely, but I'd be back to my lovely home in only a few days where I could converse in English with family while Sherra continued her work with no extended family.

I had had no idea what full-time missionaries sacrificed to serve God on foreign soil. And I probably now had only learned just a smidgen of the self-denial that came with being a full-time missionary. It was time to forget about me and think about them. Perhaps, my main purpose for this trip was to encourage, love, and lift up these missionaries.

Tomorrow I would wear a new face.

Brazil, 1985

8

God's Power over Voodoo

In America we tend to laugh at anything so bizarre as voodoo, but in Brazil we quickly learned voodoo was no laughing matter. Although Brazil is predominantly Roman Catholic, a 1980 census reported over one-half million Afro-Brazilian spiritists. This form of religion was brought from Africa by slaves hundreds of years ago. It emphasizes using potions, curses, incantations, dances, drum beating and animal (sometimes human) sacrifices.

On my third mission trip with International Crusades, voodoo quickly got my attention in Rio de Janeiro. At the beginning of a church service, my team preacher, Jim Walters, asked me to pray. Being aware of voodoo, during my prayer I voiced, "In the name of Jesus, every evil spirit present in this service must leave." I finished my prayer and sat down when Jim whispered to me that when I had commanded the evil spirits to leave, a woman slid out of her chair and onto the floor. He then told me to go take care of her.

Not accustomed to dealing with evil spirits, bewildered I asked, "But what am I supposed to do?" When he didn't answer I proceeded to go help the woman. With the help of two other women we escorted

Maria outside. Her glazed eyes indicated she seemed to be in a stupor. The women told me she often had epileptic seizures.

We sat Maria on a bench, and as I asked her questions, she glared without answering. An evil look exuded from her eyes and she seemed angry at our presence. Finally, I began to pray for her. At that, she leaped from the bench, fled around the church building and left.

Jim and I agreed we needed to do something about Maria, but we didn't know what. The book of Luke says that Jesus "gave them (apostles) power and authority to cast out demons…" and, "this kind does not go out except by prayer and fasting."[10]

The next day I determined to fast until Maria was delivered and spent the afternoon praying for her. Maria returned to church that evening and appeared to be back to normal. She told me privately that her seizures were not epilepsy, but were caused by a voodoo curse. When the man with whom Maria had previously lived joined the voodoo religion, she left him. He put a curse on her, and Maria said she didn't know what to do about it.

Exorcism was not a practice in my denomination, and, apparently, few in that church knew anything about it either. Jim and I thought maybe deliverance services were a routine happening in their church since voodoo was so prevalent in the area. Jim asked the pastor if he had cast demons out before, and he said only once, but the Sunday school teacher had done it a number of times. The pastor said that we would talk with Maria after church that night.

After church about a dozen of us sat her down, and the pastor asked if she had ever had anything to do with Macumba, the voodoo religion. Maria told us about the man who had put a curse on her five years earlier. She had experienced seizures since leaving him, and her doctor had confirmed the seizures were not epilepsy. Maria did not know we were planning to rebuke the demons in her. The Sunday school teacher took charge and commanded the demons to come out of Maria. The demons spoke many times through her. The first thing they said was, "She wants me to have her." Another time they said, "You shouldn't have burned it," apparently referring to pagan items we had burned earlier.

Four different times Maria became calm and seemed at peace. Even though she was a thin, frail person, it took six to eight men and women to hold her down, because she tried to get away. The Bible talks about demons breaking chains. It was uncanny how Maria was so strong. I was never fearful, however, for the Word clearly states that believers have authority over demons. It was the power of Jesus that gave Maria deliverance, but we were God's vessels.

After we commanded the demons to come out, Maria would go through a struggle, fighting to get away, and then she would become peaceful and quit struggling. Then we would know she was delivered of a demon. We'd sing praises to God, and a few minutes later she'd scoot down on the pew with an evil eye, and another demon would manifest itself. Then we'd go through the same thing again—rebuke the demon until it left and Maria was at peace again. Jim and I felt God told us to leave after an hour and 15 minutes, but the others worked with Maria until 4:00 a.m. We were told the next day that Maria had had a legion of demons in her, and that was why one demon after another had manifested itself.

If I had not led one person to the Lord in Brazil, the trip would've been worth it just to see Maria delivered. Her seizure had brought all of this about. It wasn't as if Jim and I were looking for demons "behind every bush." In fact, we weren't looking for them at all. It all just happened.

I don't know why the church hadn't done something before, but maybe they were afraid or didn't know what to do. Perhaps, since Jim talked to our pastor about Maria's deliverance, Jim gave them the courage to do something about it.

The next day Maria's eyes sparkled, her countenance glowed, and she was so full of love. The afternoon before we left, Maria put her hands over her face and wept profusely, because she didn't want us to go. When we left for the States, Maria cried the most, and we wept along with her.

Jim and I had another experience as we witnessed door to door. When a woman invited us into her home, Jim asked if others were there, so that we might also share with them. She shook her head no, so

Jim started to play the disco while I sat on a mat, the room's only "furniture."

Jim had played about half of the disco when a man walked through the room. Jim began to play the disco again for the man. The man, who was standing and watching Jim play the disco, suddenly stumbled backward a few steps and fell against the wall. It was as though someone had pushed him. Startled, I jumped up, and as I did, the man seemed to bounce off the first wall and fall onto the wall against where I had been resting. Jim and I watched, flabbergasted.

I believed this to be demonic, so I commanded, "In the name of Jesus, do not hurt this man." Immediately, the bouncing stopped, and the man, trembling, stood in front of me. I, too, trembled.

The word "hate" dropped into my mind, and I wondered if that might be the name of the demon. I had not experienced anything like this before, and I wasn't sure what to do. I commanded, as the pastor had done, "Demon of hate, come out of this man."

Much to my surprise the man screamed, "No! No!" over and over again. I continued to command it to come out, and eventually the man went limp, so we assumed the demon had left.

Jim and I looked at each other, stunned at what had just taken place. We prayed with the man to receive Christ, and his hardened look immediately changed to gentleness and softness. Then another word, "fear," penetrated my mind. *Was this God speaking?* I wondered. So I went through the same process, and when the demon left, the man began to weep intensely, crying out praises to God over and over. The man told us he had been given some voodoo beads and asked if we would take and destroy them, which we did.

The Lord made it clear to us on this trip, "…Don't rejoice just because evil spirits obey you; rejoice because your names are registered as citizens of heaven."[11] Just because there was activity with demons this week, we needed to keep in perspective that saving souls was the purpose for our trip. Still, I praised God for teaching us more about the power in the name of Jesus today.

Yes, curses were real. And voodoo was real. But although it was powerful, we found that the power of God's name, Jesus, was more powerful. We didn't need to fear, but rely on the power in that name which is above every other name. He was able—and still is.

*Jim Walters, Enlistment Coordinator of International Crusades,
loads up Macumba Voodoo idols belonging to a woman
who accepted Christ after being a spiritualist for 26 years.*

Burning the Macumba Voodoo idols at our host church.

Taiwan, Thailand, China, 1988

9

When God Guides, He Provides

One evening I was watching TV when a Chinese missionary, Nora Lam Sung, now deceased, told about her annual missionary tour to the Orient. I saw the mission team witnessing on China's streets and recalled my three trips to South America where thousands came to Christ. How I wished I could be a part of this missionary tour to China!

I called the 800 number to request a brochure, thinking they were signing up team members for the following summer and not for this summer. Maybe I could save up enough money for the trip by next year.

The next day I "happened" to be home on my day off work when the phone rang.

"Hello. Is this Nancy? I'm with the Nora Lam Ministries calling from California. We want you to go on the trip with us this summer."

"THIS summer?" I asked. "I thought it was for next summer." I told her I'd love to go, but there was no way, financially, that I could consider this summer. She asked me to pray about it which I agreed to do. I dismissed the trip for the time being, but considered it a possibility for the following summer.

In a few days I received the brochure, but laid it aside to read later.

One day I arrived home from work to receive quite a surprise on my answering machine.

"Hello, Nancy. This is Nora Lam, personally calling to tell you the Lord told me to call you and tell you to go on our trip this summer. Sorry I missed you. God bless you."

I was astonished, to say the least, that Nora Lam had called me. Then I decided she probably called everyone who had requested a brochure, but I was, nonetheless, thrilled.

Less than an hour passed, and I had just finished telling Joe about her call when the phone rang.

"Nancy, this is Nora Lam. I called to tell you to go on this trip. Send your deposit in tomorrow."

"I'd love to go, but I don't have the money," I answered.

"You don't have the money?" she replied. "Well, get it. Tell your friends. I'm telling you that God told me to call you and tell you to go. I don't make calls like this, but I'm being obedient to God."

My heart pounded. "Well, I'm going to have to do some heavy praying about this," I answered.

"You do that. You pray about it, and let me hear from you soon," she said..

Now what? I thought. Joe agreed I could go. He had sent me to Colombia and Brazil, but couldn't help me with the finances this time. I read the brochure, only to find that not only did the $350 deposit need to be sent immediately, but the entire fee of almost $3,000 was due in three weeks. I was overwhelmed. God would certainly have to perform another miracle like Peru, and fast, but I had learned nothing was too hard for Him.

I called Jacque Heasley, leader of my women's home cell group and asked her to pray for God's guidance. Nora Lam was a great woman of

God, and I appreciated her call, but I had to have a Word from God for myself.

After I told Jacque the story of what had just happened, she said, "Nancy, I'll pledge $50."

"Jacque, that's not why I called," I scolded. "I called for prayer."

"I know it," she answered, "but the anointing's all over me, and my heart says to give $50. I know you'll get the rest. Just talk to everyone, and I know you'll get the money."

I hung up the phone and decided to take a walk to think things through. I knew God could provide as He'd done for Peru, but was I supposed to do something this time? "God, I want to do your will," I prayed. "Please, show me what you want me to do."

"Just trust Me," came His words into my inner spirit.

Nora's words reverberated in my mind as I walked. "Tell your friends. Tell your friends. Tell your friends." Oh, how I didn't want to do that. I got so tired of receiving mail, soliciting money for a million good causes. Then the scripture came to mind, "Ask, and it shall be given to you."[12] The Lord showed me this trip wasn't for me, but for the salvation of those souls who would be reached in the Orient.

By the time I finished my walk, I had decided to go through my address book and ask God to show me to whom I should send letters. I would tell them that we would be going to Taiwan, Thailand, Hong Kong and China. We would take Bibles and witness in slums, prisons, factories, orphanages, churches of all denominations and the underground church. Many would be saved because of their contributions. I went to work on the letters.

Before mailing them, however, I went to the Bible to seek God's confirmation that I was to go on the trip. I asked the Lord to show me loud and clear if I was to go, and that He would provide. That day my daily Bible reading was Psalm 121. The words were, oh, so familiar. "I look up to the mountains—does my help come from there? My help comes from the Lord, who made the heavens and the earth."[13] I had this passage underlined and in the margin I had written, "Financial—Peru—4-27-84." Wow! That was the exact verse the Lord had given me when He paid my way to Peru. Of all the verses in the Bible that could confirm this for me, that very one "happened" to be in my Bible reading for that day.

I listened to the radio on my drive to work and heard this scripture: "But for this very purpose have I let you live, that I might show you my power, and that My name may be declared throughout all the earth."[14]

The floodgates opened as I laughed and cried at the same time, praising and thanking God for speaking so loud and clear to me. What a faithful God I serve!

I mailed about 90 letters, and when I told Joe how many letters I mailed, he said, "Honey, you'll probably receive $10,000." Immediately funds started coming in. The high point of each day was when the mail came. God knew just what I needed, and that's exactly how much I received. No more or no less. I found out later I also needed $500 for the round-trip flight to Los Angeles, but God brought that in, too.

Then the money stopped coming, just as quickly as it had started. I marveled at whom God chose to supply my need. He had done it in three weeks, and I learned, big time, that nothing is too hard for God. I was off to the Orient with Nora Lam.

Nora Lam and myself en route to Taiwan.

10

Fulfilling Nora Lam's Dream

Our mission team to the Orient consisted of 260 people from all over the USA. Years ago, as a young woman, Nora had refused to denounce her faith in God and was put before a Communist firing squad in China. As guns were shot, a bright light shone in the sky and blinded the squad. Nora was not hit, and it was evident a supernatural event had occurred.

Several years later, she and her husband, as refugees from the Cultural Revolution in 1958, fled her native Shanghai. Since then, her burning desire had been to take the gospel back to her homeland. And that's where our mission team came in.

Our first stop was at Hualien, Taiwan, where we had a three-day service outdoors. We ministered to thousands of children in the afternoons and adults at night. On our way to the children's services one day, we passed by what looked like a school. The girls wore navy skirts with white blouses and looked to be junior high school age. I asked the man sitting in front of me about the facility and I was appalled when I learned it was a rehabilitation center for prostitutes. *But they are so young,* I thought.

We heard testimonies of a man and a woman who had been raised from the dead. The man had been dead eight days while his family prayed and fasted. On the eighth day he came back to life.

The other story was of a woman who was dead on arrival at the hospital. The doctor said he could do nothing, but the woman's husband insisted he stay by her side overnight. Although he was not a Christian, he prayed, "If there is a God, give me back my wife." He prayed all night, and at 5:00 a.m. his wife sat up.

Their faith was so simple and childlike that miracles happened. We saw healings and one woman was delivered of four demons. The first night of the crusade, not only was there a sea of people as far as I could see, but it seemed they all came forward—running—to receive salvation. I had never witnessed such an awesome sight. After the services our team spread out throughout the crowd to distribute Bibles. People clutched the Bibles and wept, treasuring them deeply.

We also went to a prison to hold services. Officials told Nora she could bring in only 20 team members. But God favored Nora so much that all 260 of us went in; which was the first time in history so many missionaries were allowed in at one time. We were impressed that prisoners were being taught a trade. The prisoners were putting together tiny micro electronic parts for radios in the room where I went. The prisoners I saw looked so young, like teenagers or maybe in their early 20s, and they greeted us cordially. Their enthusiastic, happy attitudes surprised me. One young man made a cross with his fingers to let me know he was a believer.

In Bangkok, Thailand, we held services in our hotel, the Shangrila, considered to be one of the world's top hotels. At the end of the service when Nora called the team forward to pray for people, I quickly stepped out.

As I stood there, an elderly couple came toward me. Stooped over, the little woman shuffled her feet slowly, barely able to walk, as her husband supported her by the elbow.

Since we couldn't speak each other's language, the little man (both under five feet tall) pointed to the woman's legs. I assumed her legs needed healing so I motioned for her to sit down on the front row. She shuffled over to the chair and sat down. I lifted her feet up to measure her legs and found that one leg was about one-half inch shorter than the other one.

God, don't let me down now, I prayed silently.

"In the name of Jesus, I command both legs to be made the same length," I declared, and as I watched, there was a blur, then both legs were the same length. I heaved a sigh of relief with, "Thank you, Jesus," and motioned for her to stand. Then I stepped high, like I was marching and motioned for her to do the same. Her face lit up with a smile as she lifted her knees high in the air. I motioned for her to continue and, together, we marched back and forth in front of the stage. She was ecstatic, nodding her head in a bowing position over and over in gratitude, while the little man followed her around as she marched and thanked me over and over. Although I couldn't understand him, I knew he was thanking me. I nodded back and pointed heavenward, so he would know it was not me, but God who had done the healing. What a miracle working God we serve!

I thought of the lame beggar in the Bible. The beggar thought Peter was going to give him some money, but instead Peter said, "'I don't have any silver or gold! But I will give you what I do have. In the name of Jesus Christ from Nazareth, get up and start walking.' Peter then took him by the hand and helped him up. At once the man's feet and ankles became strong, and he jumped up and started walking. He went with Peter and John into the temple, walking and jumping and praising God. Everyone saw him walking around and praising God…and they were completely surprised." [15]

Peter's power did not come from within himself, but it was the power in **the name of Jesus** that healed that lame beggar. It is the same today. It was the power in Jesus' name that healed the little woman. I have the same Holy Spirit as Peter had and was only a tool. I prayed for this woman, but it was God who did the healing. What a reward to see the little woman beaming with joy as she marched! I was learning that miracles were not just a thing of the past. The power in the name of Jesus is still with us today.

*I stand with the little Thailand woman after God healed her
shuffling feet to marching like a soldier.*

11

Smuggling Bibles into China

In GA's (Girls' Auxiliary), the girls' mission organization at church, I read about missionaries smuggling Bibles into Communist China. Now, here I was, about to do it myself. I felt as though I was stepping off the pages of a mission magazine, fading into a real-life drama.

Taking Bibles into China was against the law, but bringing gifts was permissible. So Nora Lam wisely had Bibles wrapped in gift-wrap paper. As I was handed three gift-wrapped Bibles in the Hong Kong hotel, my heart raced with anticipation of delivering them into Communist China. On a spiritual high, I hugged them to my chest and sighed. I had come all the way from Texas to carry in these few Bibles. What an honor and privilege to be carrying the gospel of Jesus Christ behind the Iron Curtain.

Our hotel rooms and busses were bugged, so Nora advised us to say nothing we would not want the Communist party to hear. We used the word "bread" to refer to Bibles inside Communist territory. One wrong word could cancel our operation, defeating our purpose of taking Bibles into China.

We traveled by train from Hong Kong to Canton, China. It was a fascinating ride as we watched the Chinese in their brightly colored raincoats, wading in water-filled rice paddies. Some worked with tools while others walked behind water buffaloes.

The houses were mere shacks and apartment buildings seemed to go all the way to the sky. I counted one apartment house that rose 30 stories high. They were not apartments like we know them in the States, but were very small, with more than one family living in them many times. Some apartments were as small as a large bathroom in America. I couldn't imagine living in a space so small.

We went through a tunnel as we crossed into Communist China. Outside, on each side of the mountain was barbed wire encircling the high fence. Since we were so harmless, I thought it humorous that a Communist guard rode in each train car.

I prayed, "Lord, please take us through without any trouble." As our throng of 260 mission team members descended upon customs in Canton, China, I was thankful for my few Bibles, as I had heard some of the team hadn't received any.

We shared our Bibles with team members whom we knew hadn't received any. I would have been utterly distraught had I not received at least one Bible to carry in. After all, that had been the prime purpose of the trip, and it saddened me that some team members had no Bibles to deliver.

We separated into six lines to go through customs. Each person brought only a carry-on bag since we were staying only one night in China. As a result, we were moving through customs quickly. Much to my relief, I was waved on through without their examining my bag.

Suddenly there was a commotion in another line. Nora Lam and Mark, a team member, were in a heated discussion with a customs inspector.

"Oh, God, help us," I prayed. I knew we were in trouble.

The customs inspector had insisted Mark unwrap one of his "gifts." Mark did so, reluctantly, and the inspector became enraged when he saw the Bible. He insisted Nora tell us we could not take the Bibles into China. My heart sank. We had come so close. We were all praying for God's intervention, and Nora was not intimidated in the least. She knew God's hand was on her, and she fearlessly held her ground.

"No," she answered firmly. "You tell them."

Nora's boldness shocked me. Although we were dealing with Communists, Nora had been down this road many times. She believed that because the Communists boasted of freedom of religion in China, they wouldn't dare demand Americans leave the Bibles at customs. After all, how would that news item look flashed across American newspapers?

Also, the inspectors only assumed we all carried Bibles. They couldn't be sure because they had waved most of us through customs without inspecting our bags.

Finally, the customs chief officer was called in to handle Nora's insubordination. He was furious about the situation and was determined to prove we all had Bibles. He motioned for Gary, the next team member in line, to step forward and open up his carry-on. The terminal became deathly silent as we waited to see what would happen next.

Gary was only too happy to oblige, and much to the officer's embarrassment, he found no Bibles. Having been totally humiliated in front of his peers and 260 Americans, he muttered a few words and motioned us all on. Then, flush-faced, he wheeled around and quickly disappeared.

We wanted to shout, but we knew we had to maintain our composure. God had done it! He had set up Gary, who had no Bibles, to be at the right place at the right time. Who would've ever dreamed the person NOT carrying Bibles would be the one responsible for getting us all through?

The scripture came to mind, "My thoughts are completely different from yours," says the Lord. "And my ways are far beyond anything you could imagine. For just as the heavens are higher than the earth, so are my ways higher than your ways, and my thoughts higher than your thoughts." [16]

We were scheduled to visit ten churches in Canton, but on arrival discovered they would allow us to visit only two. Half of our group went to a church in Canton only to find when they arrived, a roadblock of dirt kept them from getting to the church. Although the group showed officials papers from Washington and argued they had a right to be there, the officials still would not allow the bus to proceed. So the team members got off the bus and started walking toward the church.

At that, the officials allowed them to pass, and men with shovels appeared out of nowhere to remove the dirt. Officials said the team could enter the church but could not preach, pray, or sing. So our team loved the people and left them Bibles.

At the house church (literally, a house), where my team attended, the pastor, Lin Xiangao, had been imprisoned for 27 years because of his faith. The perseverance of this pastor and others like him is reaping great rewards. When the Communists took over about 50 years before, there were 5 million underground Christians. When we were there in 1988, we were told there were now over 100 million Christians in China.

Our team met in the hotel dining room when we returned to Hong Kong. Referring to those on the team who had not been given Bibles to carry into China, Nora pointed her long, slender finger at us, and in broken English she passionately declared, "You see! No complain! God knows His business!"

Even though our rooms and busses were "bugged" with microphones, I was not afraid. The grace and peace of God was so real that I felt enveloped in a circle of love and protection. I believed the prayers back home had sent forth angels to be with us.

We didn't do as much one-on-one witnessing in China as we did on my other trips, but we reached out to the people through church meetings. We touched lives, showed our love and accomplished our primary goal: successfully delivering Bibles behind the Iron Curtain, thanks to God's mysterious ways. We also came home with a new appreciation for freedom of speech and religion, as well as an appreciation for the material wealth in this great U. S. of A.

* * *

(Nora Lam Sung went to be with the Lord on February 2, 2004. Her daughter, Ruth Lam Kendrick, president of Nora Lam Chinese Ministries, continues to support Christian ministries in China.)

New York, 1986

12

A Look Inside the Prison Ministry

Sharon Burton, a church friend, invited me to go to New York as her prayer partner and companion with her prison ministry. I had not been inside a prison before and looked forward to this new experience although I didn't have a clue what to expect.

Our first stop was Collins Prison, a medium-security facility. The 25-foot wire fences were topped with circled razor-edge wire that had sharp, pointed spikes on its edges. I thought, *These folks mean business.* We had to enter three gates about ten feet apart before we reached the security guard house in front of the prison.

When we got to the first gate it opened automatically. Shocked, I asked Sharon, "How did it do that?"

"They're watching us," Sharon replied.

I didn't see a soul anywhere and felt a bit on edge.

At the desk we signed in with our names, city, and purpose (prison ministry) and showed our driver's licenses. We were not allowed to take our purses in but could take only what could carry in our pockets.

I was going to take my pen, Bible, notebook, and nose spray, but was stopped since we were not allowed to take medicines into the prison. I felt a little stupid, but how was I to know? When we went through security check, the authority wouldn't let Sharon take in the tape recorder, because the security list had read, "tape player." The chaplain had to make a phone call before security would okay it. Talk about picky!

I was not exactly scared, but a little apprehensive about the unexpected so I asked prison ministry helpers to sit on each side of me in the chapel.

Sharon spoke on taking control of jealousy, resentment and bitterness in one's life. She proved to be a natural with these 50 men, and they received her graciously. Occasionally one would "Amen!" something she said or would clap. They seemed quite free and uninhibited, and their ability to express themselves helped me to relax.

I was blessed by their singing. It reminded me of the Mormon Tabernacle Choir, because their masculine voices were so strong.

After the meeting they thanked Sharon and were so appreciative to us for making the trip. The men shook my hand, too, and a couple of inmates kissed me on the cheek. I smiled, trying to be friendly and hoped my reservations didn't show. I was glad I didn't know which ones were murderers. Most of them looked just like the "boy next door." They certainly didn't look like criminals.

"All of these men are not bad guys," Sharon told me. "Some of them just made a mistake or a wrong choice in life." That helped to ease my tension, but I still didn't know which ones WERE the bad guys.

We went across the street to another part of the prison to hold another service with about 20 men. Although the singing was as beautiful, the men were not responsive at all during Sharon's talk. It was like a whole different world.

I marveled at Attica Prison with walls 30 feet high. It wasn't what I had expected a prison to look like. We went through one locked gate after another until I wondered if we'd ever get out of there. All together, we walked through 13 locked gates before we reached the auditorium that served as chapel. At each corner in back of the auditorium there was a steel cubicle with a guard in it, and a hole in the cubicles for a tear gas gun. It looked more like a castle I'd seen as a child when I lived in Germany.

I felt strange, meeting the men and asking, "How are you?" How did I think they would be, locked in prison? But they were cordial and kind. Three men almost broke my hand when we shook hands, but Sharon insisted it wasn't intentional.

We all joined hands and had an opening prayer, then sang a few choruses.

About 100 men attended, and one gave his testimony and then read John 3:16 slowly and broken. Sharon whispered that he was just learning to read. I held back tears listening to him. He had such a childlike nature that I couldn't imagine why he would be in prison.

After the service one young inmate came up to me and said his dad was a Pentecostal preacher and that's what he wanted to do when he was released. I encouraged him to follow his dream, but wondered if he was just saying that because he thought that's what I wanted to hear. Although I didn't want to be, I was skeptical of everyone. We learned there was a father and his three sons imprisoned at Attica. There were also several cases where inmates were brothers. I thought, *How sad that families waste their lives in this place when they could be doing so much for humanity and the Lord on the outside.* But I was thankful for the men who came to the services and, who, perhaps, were making a difference in the lives of other prisoners.

I didn't have the chance to lead anyone to the Lord on this trip, but my purpose had been to pray for Sharon and encourage the inmates, which I had tried to do. It had also been an eye-opener of the prison ministry and a revelation that all inmates weren't really bad guys, but that some had just made a mistake or a wrong choice in life. That one point really stuck with me and gave me a whole new outlook on the prison population. Those inmates were husbands, brothers, and fathers to people on the outside, and someone loved them just like I loved my family. And they needed Jesus—just like we all did.

This trip had shown me a new realm of the mission field, and I take my hat off to those who work day after day in the prisons.

Sometimes, I determined, going to prison was an appointment with God for many of these men.

Russia (1), 1990

13

"Go to Moscow"

I was reading my Bible one quiet morning in 1990, when the words "Go to Moscow" dropped into my mind. Startled, I looked up. It was as though someone had entered the room and spoken audibly.

Assuming it was my imagination, I passed it off. While praying later that morning, when I said, "Your will be done in my life," again the words "Go to Moscow" came to me. I knew then it was not my imagination. Glasnost had taken place only several months before, however, and Russia was not a place I wanted to be. After thinking about it for a week, turmoil filled my heart, and, I, unknowingly, was in a spiritual battle. I decided to lay the idea aside for the moment, but it continued to linger in the back of my mind.

One Sunday morning two weeks later, my pastor spoke straight to my heart. I knew then that I would go to Moscow, and peace came to my embattled spirit. I joined up with Bill Bray, a full-time missionary staff member of Christian Information Services, to take almost a half-million Bibles into Russia. Oftentimes the pastor of a church in Russia would be the only one in the congregation to own a Bible. Even hymn books were passed from generation to generation and were as precious as Bibles to the people. I learned that during the past 73 years Communists had allowed two churches in all of the Soviet Union to remain open as a token of their "freedom of religion" to the people, one Baptist, another Russian Orthodox. In Lenin's reign 3,000 priests had been murdered in one year.

The purpose of this trip was to be a "seed planter," planting the Word of God in Russia and the Ukraine. It was a revelation to me that Protestantism had never swept through the USSR. Martin Luther's Reformation went west; therefore, taking Bibles into Russia was a pioneering and history-making effort.

As our mission team awaited the connecting flight from Helsinki, Finland, to Moscow, we wandered into one gift shop after another. At a fur shop a tourist informed us that furs which cost $1,000 in America could be purchased for a mere $100 in the former USSR.

My mind began to whirl, thinking of taking home a fur jacket. I had not owned a genuine fur before, and I always admired the ladies at church with their elegant fur stoles draped about their shoulders. They looked so sophisticated and smart. Now here was a chance for me to obtain a fur and join the smart set.

Then an unwelcome thought crossed my mind. My friends and family had provided this mission trip for me. How could I go home with a fur jacket, even if it had cost only $100, and even if I had put it on my Visa? I tried to ignore the thought, because I knew this was my chance to own a fur.

As I continued to look, however, the thought wouldn't leave me alone. I recognized this nagging thought as the Holy Spirit. Now I knew why He was affectionately called the Hound of Heaven. I knew I should listen to the voice, but I didn't like what I was hearing. Finally, after momentarily having myself a pity party, I conceded.

"Okay, I won't buy a fur," I told the Lord, but I sorely regretted missing out on such a rare bargain. I reconciled, however, that God knew best as I reluctantly put my desires to rest. I knew I must refocus on the purpose of our trip—taking the gospel to Russia and the Ukraine. Texas was too hot for furs anyway, I consoled myself.

Since Russian Orthodox priests did not encourage their parishioners to read the Bible (even if they had one), even the Protestant pastors often did not recognize the importance of everyone having their own Bible. Many Russians asked for Bibles, and some kissed them and hugged them to their chests when given one. In one spontaneous prayer and praise meeting at the Pribaltiyskaya Hotel, over 250 staff and employees asked for a Bible. The Russians enjoyed our cheerful choruses (mostly scripture songs) so much that the hotel staff called in a Soviet TV crew to film the event.

Churches were being reopened almost daily and freedom of religion seemed to be coming to the USSR for the first time in history.

I was surprised at the freedom to give out Bibles. I tested it to the hilt by offering one to a Russian soldier who was guarding Red Square. He shook his head to let me know he wouldn't take it. He continued, however, to watch me pass out Bibles with no interference. Although it was permissible to give out Bibles, it was against the law to give out tracts or anything else printed which they might consider propaganda. It was also against the law for anyone under the age of 18 to join the church or for us to witness to them by handing them a tract or by witnessing to them verbally. While distributing stickers that read "Love," "Joy," and "Peace" on them, Jacque Heasley, one of our team members, was chased out of Red Square by a guard for giving out "propaganda."

I learned from a tour guide, much to my surprise, that only one in ten USSR citizens was actually a Communist. I told a young man on the street that we liked his country. He disgustingly replied, "We don't. We hate it. We'd like to leave, but we can't. The Communists have caused the morale to go down, down, down." When I told him that Jesus was the answer, he shook his head no and said Jesus might help but there was no one more powerful than the Communists.

I was amazed at USSR's religious heritage. Many crosses, icons (items of worship), and frescas (fresh plaster, paints, and crushed precious stones applied on walls) were in the museums, palaces, and cathedrals. My biggest surprise came at the Armory Museum INSIDE THE KREMLIN. There were many items that had belonged to former kings, Czars and others in power—gold crowns, gold-gilded horse carriages, thrones, chalices—ALL bedecked with crosses. When the Communists had taken over China all crosses were destroyed. I fully expected the same in Russia, and was surprised that it wasn't so.

Before the trip I had been concerned about so much sightseeing on our itinerary but learned that only "tourists," not "missionaries" could get into Russia. The Intourist, a Soviet monopoly, controlled all tourism in the USSR, and set up an itinerary we had to follow. I was glad I saw what I did, however, because it helped me understand the grief and agony of the Russian people. These educational opportunities helped us see the nation's heart before communism took over. I developed a new awareness and compassion for the Russian people.

We visited nine churches—four Baptist, four Pentecostal, and one Russian Orthodox, which represented the full denominational diversity of Russia. Our first stop was at Moscow Baptist Church, the "token" registered Baptist church.

Although the church seated 2,000, there was standing room only for the two-hour service. A beautiful pipe organ, ornate architecture and golden chandeliers were symbolic of the beauty we saw throughout the trip.

The faces of the people, however, were oppressed and empty. They would not return a smile and it was as though they were without emotions. We were later told Russian citizens were trained not to show their emotions publicly. One time we did see the Russians smile. As the congregation sang, "When the Roll is Called Up Yonder,"[17] in Russian, we Americans sang along in English. Then some of the congregation smiled, and we smiled back.

After church, we were mobbed by people wanting Bibles. Our team couldn't get onto the bus because people crowded the door wanting a Bible. We learned that many had ridden trains all night because they heard we were bringing Bibles. We left most of our Bibles with pastors to distribute. It was heartbreaking for us when someone wanted a Bible and we didn't have one to give him.

We met with a Russian Orthodox archpriest, Sergei Suzdalstsev, in Moscow who arranged for CIS to send over another 4,000 Russian Bibles. We saw many Russians repent and pray to become born-again believers. Several times we were allowed to give an American-style "altar call" and in one Leningrad suburb, 33 people came forward to receive Christ.

From Moscow we flew to Kiev, in the Ukraine. When we arrived at the underground Pentecostal church, New Life Church, church leaders immediately took our Bibles to another secret location in case the KGB decided to search the premises. The church that had served as a secret underground church prior to Glasnost and was housed in a garage on the property of church members, Aleksandra and Elsa Grushko. When we arrived at their home, the men visited outside while the women were ushered into a room to visit as dinner was being prepared.

A piano sat in one corner of the room, and after a while, with the encouragement of my team, I mustered up enough courage to meander over and check it out. When I rolled a chord I found the piano was considerably out of tune and some of the keys didn't work at all. As a pianist, my heart grieved to see a piano that could be used for God's glory, if it only worked.

While we ate outside, two KGB helicopters flew over several times. We were told to ignore them, which we did, but I must admit there was uneasiness within me throughout dinner.

I finally settled my thoughts on the underground church behind the house and awaited anxiously to enter it as I had not been in an underground church before.

The young girl in the center had been my tour guide and pregnant on my first trip, so we took baby clothes, toiletries and over-the-counter medicines for her new baby.
Ann & Jimmie Knox and myself surround the young couple.

14

The Miracle of the Red Fox Fur

After our meal the nationals and Americans gathered together in a small brick garage with a tin roof that served as the underground church. The seats were no more than wooden benches with no backs. My heart ached as I thought of my elaborately decorated church back home. We were so blessed in America. When I discovered no piano in this little church, my heart broke. I imagined if Elsa's piano was in playing condition, surely it would be put to use in this church.

Throughout the church service I couldn't keep my mind on the message as I thought of Elsa's piano. Then I forced myself back from daydreaming and listened to the sermon. Again my mind would wander, and all I could think of was the piano. I wondered how much it would cost to have it tuned and repaired. Perhaps, the sole purpose of my coming on this mission trip was to have this piano repaired.

The average monthly wage in the former USSR then was $30. I surmised that, surely, having a piano tuned would not cost more than a month's wages. As the service came to a close, I resolved to give Elsa $40 to repair her piano.

I scurried over to the interpreter, told him of my decision, and asked him to tell Elsa. He interpreted my plans to Elsa, and when he paused, I handed Elsa the money. Her eyes danced with surprised joy as she excitedly spoke to the translator while I watched. I assumed she was telling him to thank me.

The translator looked at me, smiled, and said, "She wants to give you a fox fur." Stunned by the interpreter's statement, I could only stare at him. Then I looked at Elsa and Aleksandra. They were all smiles, waiting for my answer, but my words wouldn't come. Finally the interpreter asked me again, "Would you take a fox fur?"

"Y-e- e-e-s! Y-e-e-e-s!" I stammered and nodded my head up and down so Elsa could understand.

Delighted, she grabbed me by the arm and practically dragged me out of the church to her house while Aleksandra followed closely behind. When we entered their home, Elsa skirted over to a hat rack and pulled off the most beautiful, bushy, red fox pelt I'd ever seen. Again, I was speechless. My eyes welled with tears as I thought of my dilemma in Helsinki. God knew I wanted a fur, but since I could not purchase one, I believed in His perfect and loving way, He had arranged circumstances so I could take one home after all.

When Elsa flung it around my shoulders I felt like a queen. I stroked the soft, shiny fur over and over as I flitted around, modeling it for them as we laughed together. Although we couldn't understand one another's language, it didn't seem to matter. Our communication was one of love, and right now we understood each other perfectly.

Elsa pointed at the hole in the fox's face where it had been shot. Then she pointed to Aleksandra and enacted shooting a gun. I knew she was trying to tell me that Aleksandra had killed the fox. She was so proud of her hunter-husband. When she realized I understood, she hugged me, and I pulled Aleksandra into our embrace. We stood there with our arms around one another, weeping together in the joy of the Lord. I thought, *This must be what heaven is like*, for love seemed to fill the room. I had given to them what was not a whole lot to me, but what was a fortune to them, and they, in turn, had done the same for me.

For such a serious trip, taking Bibles into the former USSR, I found it amazing God would take time to see I was given such an unnecessary gift. I thought, *Isn't that just like a father!*

How grateful I was that I had obeyed the Holy Spirit's beckoning in Helsinki. What a blessing I would've missed had I not. I was thrilled over the lovely gift of the fox fur, but the greater blessing was to have seen God's hand at work to provide it. Because of His intervention, my fox fur is much more than a beautiful possession. It is, more importantly, a symbol and testimony of God's love and grace. I thought of the scripture, "Delight yourself in the Lord; and He will give you the desires of your heart." [18]

He surely will, I thought, *and I have a red fox fur to prove it!*

Modeling my Russian red fox fur for my gracious friend.

15

Men of Faith

One of the men in the church, Oleg Tolstoy, had prayed to receive Christ while in prison. Because of his newfound faith the government had taken away his legal papers, and now that he was out of prison, he had no place to live nor would anyone hire him for work, because they feared the KGB. Oleg stayed with friends and kept on the move. He glowed with God's radiance and love, and was the happiest person I met in the USSR. Boris Zima, another church leader and our interpreter, had been in the Communist army and, while there, had given his life to Christ. Communist leaders labeled him "insane," discharged him, took his legal papers, and he could not get work either. Oleg, Boris, and our host, Pavell Suslova, were leaders of about 200 underground churches.

Zelda, our tour guide, told us the Russian history books had not been truthful about America. The pastor of a Pentecostal church told us it was difficult for him to accept us since we'd been the enemy for so long. I admired his honesty. Even if we had taken no Bibles, it would have been worth the trip just for them to see the Americans' love and concern.

We gave another tour guide, Emma, a Bible and a tract in English. The next day we asked her if she had read it. She hadn't because her husband had stayed up all night reading it. Emma and her husband, as well as Zelda, prayed to receive Christ.

This trip really helped me to realize that all of the USSR did not consist of "dirty red Communists." After coming home I'd think of Russia and would remember the empty, hungry, hurting faces that needed the love of God so badly. But I also remembered the joy of the Lord on the Russians who were believers. This period of Glasnost had given them real hope.

My hope was that maybe those churches we ministered in would have a different opinion of us "dirty Yankees" and realize there were believers across the world who loved them and were praying for them. And I hoped that the Bibles we took would touch souls and change lives to provide hope that only God could bring.

Russia (2), April, 1991

16

Bibles and Peanut Butter for Russia

After returning from my second mission trip to the former USSR in 1991, people asked me if the food lines seen on TV news were as bad as they seemed.

"Without a doubt!" I exclaimed. Food rationing peaked with a mere one and a half pounds of meat allowed each person per month. I asked our tour guide how they survived and learned that potatoes were their mainstay.

Led by Max Wilson, a layman from Mason, Texas, 11 pastors and laypeople spent ten days in Moscow, Leningrad, and in Kiev of the Ukraine.

No nationals we talked with supported Mikhail Gorbachev, and everyone seemed bitter toward the government. They said their government was selling them foodstuffs that had been donated by other countries and the people questioned what the money was being used for.

One woman who invited us for dinner explained that Germany had contributed most of our meal to her church. The church had then distributed the food to its church members.

We visited in the home of one of our interpreters, Vasili, who lived in an elegant four-story house that had been built and owned by Vasili's great-grandmother before the revolution. Communists had confiscated the house, and now Vasili and his mother lived in only two rooms of the house, and shared a kitchen with three other families who lived on the same floor. Sixteen families now lived where at one time only one family had resided.

We took Bibles, foodstuffs, clothes, and medical supplies on this trip. The Russian people enjoy peanut butter, which is unavailable in Russia, so much that they jokingly say, "One can buy the Kremlin for a jar of peanut butter." We took Bibles for the heart and peanut butter for the stomach.

We visited a children's hospital in Kiev where cancer victims from the Chernobyl nuclear leak were housed. I was unsure of possible radiation exposure and hesitated going in, until God reminded me in Psalms 91 that, "No plague shall come near your tent."[19] Having been reminded of God's steadfast protection over me, I went gladly.

Twenty-two children congregated in a meeting room with their mothers where we distributed Bibles, crayons, toys, and clothes. We also handed out bubble gum, which was unavailable in Russia at that time and much coveted by the children.

Seeing the hopelessness in the mothers' eyes broke our hearts. Max had firmly stated, "You cannot cry!" Our forced smiles helped us fight back the tears. Our purpose was to leave with them hope and faith that with God, all things are possible, even the healing of their children.

Ivan Lefchuk, a Russian Christian pastor, told of his being beaten while in prison for his faith. The prison guards cut the bottom of his feet from one end to the other so he could no longer walk, and dumped him in a field outside the prison. He had been beaten so badly and had so many broken bones the guard thought he was dead.

Pastor Lefchuk said that as he lay in the field dying, Jesus appeared to him, and told him he was healed and that in a short time he would be free to have his own church. God touched Pastor Lefchuk and miraculously healed him completely. He jumped up and ran back to the prison, where the guards fell on their knees when they saw him alive. He told the guards to gather the people, which they did, and 5,000 inmates and guards gave their lives to Christ. Pastor Lefchuk was set free and given a church building within a month.

We held services in a high school auditorium where 200 teenagers gathered to hear the Word of God. Max accompanied us with his guitar as we sang mostly scripture songs. Max told of the saving faith in the Lord Jesus and invited the teens to give their lives to God.

One young man later told me it was difficult to believe there was a God when they had been taught atheism all their lives. However, 90 percent or more raised their hands to receive Christ. We were astounded. The principal, who also attended the meeting, invited us back, and was delighted when we offered to leave Bibles and tracts for his 40 teachers. We explained that we'd leave all the Bibles we had and didn't know if we had enough for all the teachers, but when we counted them, to our surprise, we had exactly 40 Bibles. To see God go before us as we ministered continually amazed me.

We visited New Life Church that I had attended on my first trip, and found it had quadrupled in size in only one year. The pastor had spent 27 years in prison and his church members had spent an average of four years each in prison for following Christ. As one Russian woman prayed over me with such power in a church service, I asked myself, *Who do we think we are, coming to witness to these people?* Their faith, their prayers, and their power with God made ours seem so elementary.

We could learn a lot from the Russian believers about faith, but there were yet those who did not know of God and His love, and that's why we went—to take Bibles, to show our love, and, once again, to let them know there were those across the world who cared.

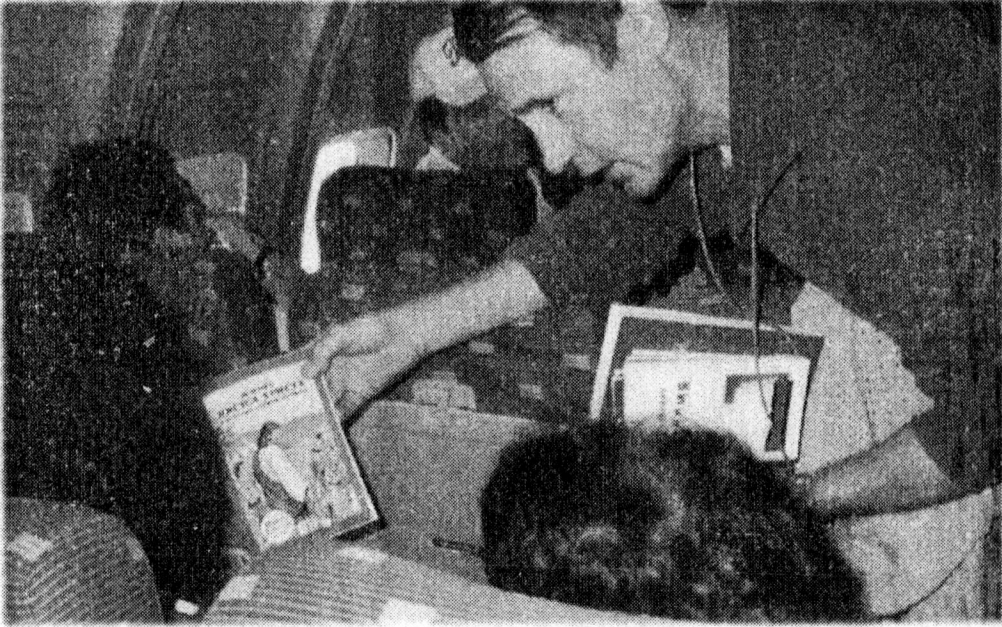

Max Wilson, our team leader from Mason, TX,
gives a Bible to a Russian family on the plane as we head home.

17

Hearing the Heart Cry of Russia
(*The Russian Coup*)

It finally happened. I thought it probably would someday—
Communists taking power again in Russia. Many thought democracy
wouldn't last there; it had been too good to be true.

As I watched television at home and saw thousands of Muscovites
in the crowd around the Parliament building in Moscow, I began to
weep.

"What's wrong, honey?" Joe, my husband, asked.

"They've already been through so much suffering," I sobbed.

After my mission trips to the former USSR, where I personally
heard so many tales of suffering, I was no longer watching events
unfold as a stranger would.

I thought of the New Life Church in Kiev, Ukraine, that had been an
underground secret church before Glasnost. I could imagine the
congregation when it heard about the Communist coup. Most of the
church members had tasted freedom for the first time in their lives these
past two years.

I thought of Emma, our tireless, dedicated Russian interpreter. She
and her son had immigrated to America since Glasnost, but left her
husband behind to care for his sick, aged mother. He had hoped to join
Emma here someday. Would he ever be able to leave the USSR now?
The Moscow airport was reported to be closed.

It seemed that God had raised the Iron Curtain for but a moment. One reason, I believed, was so the gospel could be preached and Bibles could be distributed. Another reason, I believed, was to allow the thousands of Jews to leave the former USSR and return to their homeland as a fulfillment of end-time prophecy. Many Jews had left Russia for Israel.

We had carried almost a half-million Bibles into the former USSR on our first trip. Now that Communists had taken over, it seemed like a dream that I ever went. A moment in history when the veil lifted, by the grace of God I had been privileged to glimpse behind the Iron Curtain.

Only months before, we had freely distributed Bibles at Red Square, where now Communist tanks stood guard. Could this really be happening?

Then I wondered about the Americans and visitors from other countries who were guests in the former USSR now, perhaps there to distribute Bibles as we had done. I wondered about their safety and prayed for God's protection over them.

In the beginning of Glasnost, many questioned the validity of true freedom in the USSR. I, too, had thought maybe it was some kind of Communist trick, but after a few months began to accept that Glasnost might be real. The travel agency had assured our mission team would be safe. I had wondered at the time how they could be so sure.

I thought of the beautiful, ornate onion-domed Gospel Temple in Leningrad (now St. Petersburg). For the past 70 years it had been used as a factory and warehouse. At the beginning of Glasnost, the State had given it back to the people. On my first trip to the former USSR, a few months after the initiation of Glasnost, only the stage of the church had been restored. By my second trip, almost a year later, the entire first floor had been renovated—all from monetary gifts of love. I wondered if the Communists would again seize this temple that was dedicated to the continuation of Christianity.

Although I had visited several countries in South America and the Orient, no people had gained my compassion like the Soviets. A pathetically hopeless people, they had longed for freedom. Such a hunger for the Word of God I had never seen before. I thought how the seed of Christ's saving knowledge had been planted. Grown men and women would rush toward us, sometimes running to receive a gospel tract. To many, that was their only touch with the living Word of God. Now, at least they had that.

I thought of the Soviets' economic needs, vast as they were. On my last trip to Russia our driver had dropped us off at church and informed us he'd be back to pick us up several hours later. He needed to buy gasoline, and by paying a higher price, he could purchase it within about three to four hours. He told us that during the past winter there had been a 12-hour wait for gasoline. Even during our gasoline wars in the States, we had not experienced anything like that.

After I went to bed, thoughts of Russia continued to whirl in my mind. An hour and a half later I still lay awake. As particular Soviet friends came to mind, I lifted them to God and eventually, dozed off.

The next morning, due to lack of sleep, I stumbled around trying to get ready for work. Thoughts of the USSR continued to plague me as I dressed. I could think of little else. And I prayed.

Later that morning, on the car radio, a newscaster announced, "The Communist coup committee that sought to overthrow President Mikhail Gorbachev has disbanded and is fleeing Moscow."

"Thank you, God!" I shouted, elated at this fantastic news. I found this news almost as difficult to believe as I had that the Communists had held Mr. Gorbachev under house arrest.

How grateful I was to live in America! Even though America seemed to be at an all-time low, morally, we still had our freedom. And we had grocery stores filled with all the food we could buy. And it didn't take a combined family income of two or three generations to purchase a car after a seven-year wait. And we could worship freely without KBG helicopters encircling above our churches to investigate.

The statue of Lenin had been torn down. Church was now being held in a KGB building, and Russian propaganda presses were now printing Bibles. The USSR had been freed once more, but we didn't know what tomorrow would hold for them.

I remembered a war not so long ago called "Desert Storm." I was fully convinced that prayer power, not gun power, had won that war. And prayer power could win the war for democracy in the USSR.

We must hear the heart cry of the Russian people, I thought. *We can help keep their country free. We not only can; we must.*

Russia (3), November, 1991

18

Learning How to Wait on God

The opportunity arose for me to go on a third mission trip to Russia, but again there were no funds available. What to do? So I went to God in prayer. He assured me I was meant to go.

When I asked what I should do to finance the trip, the words "Nothing. Absolutely nothing" came into my inner spirit.

What? How could God supply my need if no one knew about it? On my last three mission trips I had written letters to request contributions, and each time I was amazed how the exact amount needed came in.

But to do nothing was just about the most difficult thing the Lord could ask of me. How could I sit back and wait for the money to come in out of nowhere? But to do nothing was precisely what I believed the Lord was telling me.

So, impatiently, I did nothing except tell a few close friends and my Sunday school class about it, because I needed prayer for peace. I also requested prayer that the person or persons who were to provide my way would be sensitive to the leading of the Holy Spirit. When I told a friend about this trip, I told her I wished God would have a complete stranger pay for it just to show me He didn't need my help.

Later, however, I 'fessed up and asked the Lord to forgive me for telling a soul. Telling about the trip only showed my lack of faith that God would provide. This test reminded me of my Peru experience, but it seemed harder this time. I wasn't as sure that I was meant to go this time. One day I was up, the next day, down. How thankful I was for the mustard seed of faith spoken about in the Bible and I hoped I had that much.

One night God awakened me and told me to get out of bed and get down on my knees. As I knelt, immediately God spoke in my spirit, "I have not brought you confusion, but I have brought you direction. Proceed as with Peru. Proceed as with Peru. Proceed as with Peru. Proceed as with Peru."

Peace was mine, and I crawled back into bed, grateful for a patient Father.

The next day, however, doubts again clouded my mind. Even though at times my faith faltered, I could still proceed as with Peru in obedience and wait for God to act. I mailed in my money for the visa and packed. I could do nothing to raise the money. The ball was definitely in God's court.

When I came home from a meeting a couple of weeks before departure to Russia, I noticed something scribbled on my bathroom mirror. Joe had never done anything like that before, and as I moved closer there was a message written in lipstick. I snickered at Joe's ingenuity. He knew he'd be asleep when I got home and apparently had wanted me to get the message that night.

I walked closer to read, "Max (mission team leader) has your money!"

It was all I could do to keep from shouting, but I didn't want to awaken Joe. My ticket was paid for, and I was on my way. God had done it again!

As it turned out one of our team members, Jan Adair, was planning some home repairs. When the job bid came in much lower than expected, she and her husband, John, aware of my need because Max had requested prayer from all the team for my financial miracle, graciously agreed to pay my entire way.

As an added blessing, God had honored my wish that the trip would be paid for by a COMPLETE STRANGER. And to top it off, my gracious contributor turned out to be my roommate on the trip.

And some say God is dead.

19

Trusting God Moment by Moment

It seemed that obstacles were plentiful on this trip to Russia. On past trips we had joked about "suffering for Jesus" when we had no hot water. We drank from cracked cups and glasses with chipped rims in the hotels, and in spite of the fact that everyone got sick on the trip at one time or another, we did have warm rooms. Regardless of the inconveniences, we believed that our mission was going to be accomplished by the grace of God.

I joined the team in Austin's airport and was introduced to Anna Lubkova, age 75, (going on 16—she walked eight miles a day!) She was formerly from Russia and had served as a nurse in the Soviet Army. Captured by the Germans, she was placed in a prisoner of war camp, where after the war, she was freed by the Americans. Anna immigrated to America and had lived here ever since. She became a beloved friend and proved to be one of the most remarkable people I ever met.

In Rostov, one of the cities on our agenda, Communists assassinated the family of Anna's husband. Returning to Russia for the first time in 50 years proved to be painful, but Anna was a trooper. She served as our interpreter, helping tremendously, and her testimony of her love and belief in God proved to be a blessing to the Soviets, many of whom had believed there was no God.

Our first big obstacle came at the Austin airport when our team of nine showed up with 66 pieces of boxes and luggage, about 3,000 pounds overweight. We missed our plane while dealing with authorities. They reduced the overweight charge somewhat, but since only two of our team had paid for their own trip, the amount was still out of reach.

Fortunately, a few people from Austin churches who were at the airport to see us off came to our rescue and provided the needed funds. Truly a miracle. All the way we had overweight problems. At customs in Moscow they did not want us to bring in our boxes at all. After Max Wilson, our team leader, opened some boxes and gave Bibles and tracts to the airport personnel, they sought out the customs "head honcho," who eventually allowed us to take our boxes through. Another miracle of God! As we loaded up, Max declared, "I'm just a suitcase carrier for God!"

I laughed and responded, "Hey, Max, that would be a great name for a book, and I just might write it someday!"

What a privilege it was to room with Jan Adair, the "complete stranger," who had paid for my trip. Her giving spirit was evident throughout the mission. She gave her newly purchased boots to an 18-year-old girl whose mother told us a pair of boots cost one year's salary. The girl had been exposed to the Chernobyl nuclear incident and had many headaches and continued to lose weight. We prayed for God to intervene with her health and make her whole again.

We took Bibles, songbooks, Christian literature, food, medicine and clothing for the churches. With winter at hand, we focused on providing gloves and socks as well. And of course, we took the much-desired peanut butter.

One would think that a trip such as ours would have had a set itinerary, but that isn't always the case. We arrived in Rostov without knowing a soul or a contact there. Our purpose had been to take a bus two hours south from Rostov to Krasni Sulin and meet a pastor with whom Max had corresponded. Max, however, was not sure the pastor had received his letter notifying him of our plans, so Max sent a telegram to let him know we had, indeed, arrived.

Max declared, "We must walk by faith and expect God to open doors for us." That afternoon in our hotel lobby Max met two young men who were students at a "building engineers" university. They wanted us to come to their university to speak.

They obtained an invitation for us the following afternoon. As the young college students entered the room, the teacher apologized to us for their stares. She informed us that they had never seen Americans before.

Max played his guitar as we sang throughout the trip, but one day he accidentally left it in a taxi, and that was the last he saw of it. Because he led singing with the guitar, my piano playing had not been needed, but as we entered the classroom there sat a piano. Max asked if I would play it as we sang. How I relished playing the piano on the mission field. I was sorry Max had lost his guitar, but I welcomed the opportunity to play the piano for the rest of the trip.

Max, who speaks fluent Russian, told of God's love and salvation and that they could be saved from their sins. He spoke at length, wanting his words to be very clear and simple so they might understand. After his message Max asked how many wanted to receive Christ, and the entire class of 80, less one young man who claimed to be an atheist, raised their hands. They were hungry to know about God, but there had been no one to tell them.

Max explained the salvation message again to make sure they understood. And once more, all 80, less the atheist, raised their hands. So Max led them in a salvation prayer.

This event, planned by God alone, proved to be the most successful of our trip. Max again reminded us that when we trust God, He directs our steps. It is a lesson we learned time after time on this trip.

Taking over where Max left off.

20

Interviewing Russians About the Coup

This trip was shortly after the coup in Russia, and I was anxious to hear of the people's reaction. Were they glad Communism had returned or not?

I asked Gertie Levchenko, a teacher in a Christian school, to tell me her story. When the coup happened, she was on vacation, visiting friends in the country.

"It was very interesting," she said. "We had breakfast, and my children and I went for a morning walk. I switched on the radio set, but there was only classical music and no other events on any station. Every Russian person knows if there is classical music on, somebody is dead.

"Then the music was interrupted by a narrator who announced, 'Attention! Listen to what we say.' Then he began to read the laws of a new government, and it was awful. All our neighbors were in horror because we understood at once that it would be very bad for us. It may be worse than in Stalin's time. What was worse was that some people were glad. That was worst of all. We began to listen to the radio, but we couldn't receive any truthful information, only from BBC (England station), because our Russian radio and TV gave us no truth.

"I read on our Christian calendar that all we receive in life is from God, and I became very quiet, because I believed at once that this situation was from Him. I took this calendar to the house of my friend and began to read the Holy Words and explain to them that we must receive this situation as being from Him in order that we might have victory. They didn't understand, however, because they were Jews and were afraid the new government would punish them because they were Jews.

"They asked questions such as, 'Why did God punish us? What have we done? Why is He so cruel to our country?' It was so awful. They didn't want to believe that this situation was from Him.

"After the coup was over, it was wonderful on the radio. The announcers interrupted each other saying, 'We are free! How wonderful!' They wanted to tell us how they took part in the events and were very excited. They apologized for not telling us the truth. They hadn't wanted to say, 'Everything is okay,' during the three days, but some narrators had been punished for telling the truth. So the government found narrators who would lie for them.

"Our weapon to keep us from being afraid was prayer," Gertie continued.

"Do you think the Communists will take over again?" I asked her.

"My father is still a Communist in his heart," she answered. "Communism is now forbidden, but in their hearts, many are still Communists. I don't think communism will take over again, because our government (Mikhail Gorbachev) understands the principle of communism which is anti-god. The main principle of communism is hatred, and it's caused a battle between my father and me."

"Does your father think the Communists will take over again?" I asked.

"He's not sure," Gertie answered. "He was very glad about the rebellion."

The Communists rewarded her father with food and many gifts because he was loyal. Communists could go to different shops than the average person to purchase food, clothing and other items. Even though only ten percent of the Russian people were Communist, since the Communists' government had been in control, all people had to follow their demands.

"Is your family getting enough food?" I asked Gertie.

"No, Yeltsin says the prices must be very high. Many shops don't sell anything, because they want to sell at an expensive price. Yeltsin gave the plan to charge more for items, but no one can afford them. Food is still in the few Communist shops that are in secret places. The government people still eat well, but not the average person. There is no butter, cheese, no vegetable oil, no eggs or meat. We survive on potatoes and spaghetti.

"For breakfast we eat grated carrots with sugar, tea and bread. For lunch we eat milk soup with spaghetti. For dinner we eat potatoes, bread, cabbage and tea. There is plenty of bread. Sometimes we can buy beets and onions. Sixty percent of the population in the former USSR live below poverty level."

* * *

Helene Suslova, age 27, worked in Rostov at an Intourist Hotel when the coup took place. She had been lying on the beach and was shocked and horrified. "I knew the coup wouldn't last, because our people had experienced too much," she said. She hadn't known what to do, so she went to a telephone station and called her parents. The BBC (England radio station) announced that tanks were only in Moscow and Leningrad. No information was available on the Russian radio stations.

"How did you feel when the coup was over?" I asked.

"I cannot express it in words," Helene answered, indicating it was too wonderful. "I prayed to God in my own words, because I did not know any prayers. I go to church one time a month at the Nativity Church, the only church not destroyed in the city during the 70 years of the Communist Party."

* * *

In my hotel lobby I heard a Russian man speaking English, so I asked if I could interview him about the coup. Vladimir Gitin, age 51, from Rostov on Don, worked as a scientist at the Institute of Neurocybernetics. He was at work when the coup took place and said,

"It was really a great shock! I tried to estimate the future, to predict the coming steps. I don't believe in prayer and did not pray. I respect those who are believers, but myself, I do not pray. The Soviet radio gave no objective information, only about the coup for 24 hours a day. They gave the same news, over and over again. I feared that communism was back to stay."

When asked what he did when he heard about the coup he answered, "I wanted to go to Moscow to defend the people, but I couldn't get a ticket. I called a friend in Moscow, and he told me where the tanks were, that this was very serious."

Gitin said there was a large demonstration in Rostov that he participated in to support Yeltsin. He carried a banner that read, "Yeltsin, Yes!"

Gitin said no one was hurt in the demonstration, that it was peaceful, because everyone felt the same way, including the policemen.

Gitin was at work when news came over the radio that the coup had been defeated, and everyone cheered and celebrated with cake and tea.

When I explained the plan of salvation to Gitin, he smiled at "my ignorance." I asked if he had a Bible, and he said that he had several, that they were "good historical books."

"Every culture has its religion," he continued.

I asked if he died that night would he go to heaven or hell, but he smiled and said that he had no need of that. He believed in nature only, and after he died, there would be nothing. His spirit would die with him. It was obvious I was getting nowhere so we exchanged addresses, and I thanked him for his time.

After interviewing a few others I found no one who had wanted to go back into communism. All had rejoiced over the coup's defeat. At least now maybe the former USSR would continue to be free so the Word of God could go forth in this lost nation

On our last night in Russia, as we rode the bus for one and a half hours from the airport to our hotel, Moscow had its first snowfall of the season. We were so tired by this point, it was as though God gave us this beautiful moment to lift our spirits. As we made the long trek to our hotel, I moved away from the others and sat on the back seat of the bus by myself, to sing praises to God, and marveled once more that He allowed me to be part of such a glorious trip. The roar of the bus drowned out my singing, so I cut loose and sang to my loving Lord of His glory and power and love and mercy. I rejoiced that I was a "King's Kid," that my steps were ordered by Him, and that He had given me the privilege of sharing His love one more time in Russia.

Latvia, 1993

21

A Displaced People in Their Own Country

Although 50,000 armed Communist troops still occupied Latvia, a former republic of the USSR, the people of Latvia were allowed to come and go freely since Glasnost. Since the 14th century, Latvia had been under the rule of the former USSR, Poland or Germany, having been free only 24 years during that time.

Russian troops were scheduled to leave the country in June 1993, but there was one big problem. Many Russians called Latvia home and didn't want to leave. Since the former USSR had occupied Latvia since 1940, many Russians knew the country as their only home, yet they were unwelcome and hated by the Latvia nationals.

Latvia was inhabited by only 30 percent natives while Russians and other allies compiled the remaining population. The Latvians were really a displaced people in their own country.

In the spring of 1993 I journeyed to Latvia for a nationwide evangelistic crusade with IC. The local church was supposed to make appointments for witnessing before we arrived, but because of past persecutions of Christians by the Communists, most were reluctant to open their homes to strangers.

With so many years of communism, where no one dared to tell even one's family he was a Christian, the church's knowledge of "outreach" was nonexistent. There was also the possibility that communism would return and many didn't want to risk labeling their homes as Christian for fear of possible future persecution.

Most witnessing was done in over 100 public schools where we were welcomed by staff and students. Our 22-year-old Latvian crusade organizer at my church said she had purchased no clothes or basic needs in three years. When we insisted on providing her aid, the first item she requested was an umbrella, an absolute necessity in Latvia. Fortunately, we had brought several for gifts.

Well-made, hardback Bibles were easily accessible in Latvia bookstores for $2.

One of our mission team members, Adam, had left his native country of Latvia 46 years before. His dream was to return home to a free country. That dream was fulfilled on this trip. He had served in the Latvian army during World War II, when his entire regiment broke through the lines and pleaded with the American army to take them, which they did.

Shortly afterwards, 40,000 Latvians were banished to Siberia. Somehow, Adam discovered his name had been listed among those scheduled to be exiled where people worked outside in temperatures of -49 degrees. At -50 degrees prisoners were allowed to stay indoors.

Another man who had been exiled to Siberia told us that every morning where he was held prisoner, from 25 to 30 prisoners would die from exposure to the bitter cold.

Pastor Gunars, now deceased, related a fascinating story. Nine years before, during the Communist regime, he and four pastors were meeting when they were alerted the KGB was coming. Pastor Gunars went outside to pray when God audibly spoke to him.

"Who do you fear, man or Me?" came the audible voice.

"You, Lord," Pastor Gunars answered.

"Don't be afraid," commanded the voice.

Pastor Gunars said all his fear left and when the KGB demanded to see his passport, God blinded their eyes so they could not read his name. Also a stack of Bibles sat on the desk directly in front of the KGB, but, miraculously, they did not see them. The KGB left without arresting anyone.

At that time Pastor Gunars had just organized his first church. During the Communist regime he organized and preached at seven churches.

Although our mission team went to minister, we recognized that it was we who were blessed. As we looked forward to the next trip, the big question always was, would the doors still be open?

Russia (4), 1994

22

God Puts Together a Mission Team

It was about time to drag those suitcases out of the attic again, tuck in a few clothes and fill the suitcases with gifts of medicines, food, and other items so needed in Russia, and head off on another mission trip.

Months back when I had learned of International Crusades' plans for this mission trip to Russia, I somehow had an inkling I'd be on that plane. I also sensed in my spirit that a team was to go from my church. I told no one about my feelings except Joe, and we prayed.

One morning in church, however, I began to wonder if God really wanted me to go or if it was just Nancy Gayle desiring to go. So I asked Him to give me one sign to confirm His intentions, because I wanted to be in His perfect will. I had no idea how He would do it, or if He would do it.

That night before church, Nancy Corley, the leader of our church's puppet ministry, came up to me and asked if I had a minute, to talk.

"Nancy," she said nervously, "God has been dealing with me for several weeks to talk to you about something." She spoke so seriously that I wondered if I had offended her. She continued, "I think He wants me to take a particular puppet to Russia." Although she knew I had been there before on mission trips, she knew nothing of my current plans for going to Russia.

When she said "Russia," it reverberated over and over in my mind, "Russia! Russia! Russia!" and my heart began to pound. I knew then that God was speaking, telling me to go to Russia. God had not only given me confirmation, but here was the second team member. That meant it was God's will for us to take a team from our church. I burst into tears.

"Nancy, I'm going to Russia in June!" I blurted out. We excitedly discussed the trip a bit, and as the service was about to begin, I darted over to our pastor, Dr. Bob Price, to ask if I could give a quick testimony about what had just happened, to which he agreed.

I told the congregation what had just taken place and issued an invitation to anyone who might want to go on our church mission team to Russia.

I asked the Lord if there was anyone in particular I should talk to. The only name that came to mind was Mary Nan Foster. She had not been on a mission trip before, and I didn't know her well as she was new in our church.

One Wednesday night in church several of us were discussing the trip, and Mary Nan happened to be sitting there. I asked her, point blank, if she'd like to go. Usually a person would hem-haw around with an answer, but she shocked me when she answered quickly and boldly, "Yes!" She said she didn't have the money, but we both knew that if God wanted her to go, He would provide. That was the kind of response I liked to hear.

One evening Joe and I were invited to dinner with Mona and Dennis Rumbo. They had recently joined our church and had recommitted their lives to the Lord. Joe was their deacon, and Dennis had shared with him how he was looking for new ways to serve the Lord. As we discussed the matter over dinner, Joe suggested that Dennis go on a mission trip with IC and that He might consider the upcoming trip to Russia. Dennis reared back in his chair and burst into laughter. He bellowed in his East Texas drawl, "I'm not going to Russia! That's not one place I'd like to be right now."

A seed was planted, however, and I asked IC to send Dennis the registration packet.

In due time, Dennis was the next person to sign up for the trip. This was only the beginning of what God had in store for Dennis, as he eventually served IC as vice president of African ministries for the entire continent of Africa.

I mailed letters to friends and family about my trip, telling them we were putting together a team and if anyone felt led to go with us, to let me know. Immediately Teri Caswell, a former member of our church who had moved to another town, called me. She knew God was calling her to go in spite of the fact she didn't have the finances or a baby-sitter to care for her preschooler, but she was assured that God would take care of her needs.

How exciting it was to see God put the team all together, one by one. Walking with God got more and more exciting.

About 100 teams were to be scattered over Russia at the continental divide of Europe and Asia. We had been informed that these rural towns were raised for the sole purpose of making ammunition and warfare, and that they were 150 years behind our culture.

We were told that married women must wear a scarf on their heads at all times; we could wear no cosmetics, slacks or jewelry except for our wedding rings; and we were instructed not to smile in public since Russians were private with their emotions.

Although it was my fifth mission trip to the former USSR, it was the first time I'd be staying in a home of Russian people. Our Cornerstone Team was all set and ready to go.

Our Cornerstone Baptist Church Team, (L to R) Me, Teri Caswell,
Dennis Rumbo, Nancy Corley, and Mary Nan Foster.

23

Fighting a Battle for My Health

I was into my fifth week with pneumonia, and departure for Russia #4 was only two weeks away. My chances to go looked slim, but I was believing for a miracle. God had touched me and healed me instantly numerous times, and I knew He could do it again.

I had been improving until I overdid it and had a relapse. It only made my chances of going look worse. After taking four rounds of antibiotics and not seeing much improvement, I decided to change doctors. Mary Nan Foster told me how her doctor, Dr. Christine Walker, gave antibiotic shots daily for a quick healing. I certainly needed a quick healing, so I decided to give her a try. Time was running out.

Joe was hesitant about me making this trip after my long bout with pneumonia, but I knew God had called me. So Joe and I made a pact that if I wasn't completely well on June 15, a week before we left for Russia, I wouldn't go. That weighed heavily on my mind. I knew God could heal me in an instant, and I couldn't believe He didn't want me to go on this trip. I was sure He had called me to go, and already almost all the needed funds were in.

I hadn't been concerned about the funds at all this trip. God had brought in the need on so many trips that I knew He would take care of it again. I reckoned that since Satan couldn't bombard me about the finances this time, he keyed in on my health. Fighting for my health had been a tougher fight than waiting on money to come in.

During the wee hours of June 9, I turned to my Psalms for that particular day. There it was! My word from God, already highlighted in orange.

"He will not abandon them to the power of their enemies. The Lord will help them when they are sick and will restore them to health." [20]

First of all, the part about abandonment really spoke to me, and naturally the part about healing was exactly what I needed. I got so high spiritually I couldn't go back to sleep until 5:00 a.m. I knew then I'd make that trip. I was on shoutin' ground.

I started on the antibiotic shots from the new doctor on Thursday but was still so weak on Friday that I asked my friend LaDonna to take me to my doctor appointment. By Saturday I could drive myself, although Joe offered to take me. Then by Sunday I felt almost well. I could see then that I was going to make it. I was so excited that I shouted all over the house.

That afternoon at my grandson's baptismal service I told his pastor about my need for a miracle of healing. There were only three days left until June 15, Joe's and my pact day. Before the baptismal services the church prayed for me, and the Holy Spirit ministered to me so powerfully that I became limp. Even after we got home I could still feel the presence and power of the Holy Spirit. I was excited to be able to go back to my church Sunday night. After so many weeks of illness I was hungry for church.

Monday morning, however, brought devastation. I woke up feeling miserable. My throat hurt, and I couldn't stop coughing. I hadn't coughed in three weeks, and I knew I'd never make it by Wednesday, just two days away. Apparently I had overdone it on Sunday, and I remembered we had sat under the air condition vents at church Sunday night when the cold air had blown on us throughout the service. I simply could not handle another relapse. I was sick and tired of being sick and tired.

I finally went to the Lord and released the trip to Him. I believed deep down in my spirit that I was to go on that trip, but I couldn't make myself well. I would have to honor the pact I made with Joe in two days. At this point I didn't even know how to pray, but I told Him I was willing to do what He wanted. I would be greatly disappointed if I didn't go, but He knew best.

Several people had suggested that maybe God didn't want me to go. I just couldn't buy into that, because I was so sure He had called me. I truly believed all this sickness was harassment from the enemy, as every one of our church team who was going on the trip had been sick the past week. I gave the situation to the Lord and tried to leave it there.

Mary Nan had had pneumonia five times and told me it takes weeks to get over pneumonia, that one doesn't get well in a day like with a virus. So I decided to get back to the shots and made an appointment. I asked Dr. Walker at what point would it be safe to make this trip?

She looked at me puzzled and said, "Well, I think it's safe now. Let me listen to your lungs."

"Your lungs are great!" she announced.

I couldn't believe her words. *Oh, ye, of little faith,* I thought. She explained that my coughing and throat problem had nothing to do with my lungs, and she told me I didn't need to take any more shots. *Russia, here I come!* I thought.

All the way home I shouted, sang and boo-hooed at God's faithfulness. I called my family to tell them the good news. By the afternoon my throat and cough weren't nearly as bad as when I'd awakened.

Once more, God did not abandon me, but healed me. The devil lost again. I thought of the scripture that reads, "The Lord will work out His plans for my life,"[21] and "You chart the path ahead of me."[22]

He had made a way where it seemed to be an impossibility, and I could pack my bags. This suitcase carrier was hitting the road again.

24

God Speaks Through a Rainbow

Shortly before our trip to Russia, TV news reporters warned the public of the dangers of flying on Aeroflot, Russia's only national airline at that time. One Aeroflot airliner had recently crashed because a pilot's son had been at the controls.

Regardless of the warning, our mission team was scheduled to fly 1,000 miles on Aeroflot from Moscow to Perm. Of my ten mission trips, I was more concerned about this flight than any other I'd made.

As I boarded Aeroflot I prayed for God's protection. I tried not to worry, but it was easier said than done. I knew this trip was God's will for my life. I found my seat and was glad to be seated by the window. Maybe I could get some shut-eye after the long haul from Dallas to Moscow. I had slept only four hours the night before. As the airplane lifted off, I took a deep breath and prayed, "Okay, God. Your will, not mine."

The jetliner rose higher and higher until we were above the clouds and then it circled around. As it did, I saw the right wing dip down, and my eyes fell on the airplane's tiny shadow on the glowing white clouds.

Then suddenly to my amazement a rainbow appeared, encircling the airplane's shadow. I gasped, spellbound, as I had never seen a circular rainbow before. The color was spectacular, and I watched for a moment before grabbing for my camera. When I looked back to take a picture, however, the airplane had leveled off, and to my disappointment, the shadow and rainbow were gone.

As I thought of the rainbow, I remembered how only a year ago a loving friend, Patsy Sanders, had faced a bone marrow transplant to try to overcome leukemia. Brother Bob, our pastor, had stated in a sermon that to have a rainbow, there first must be rain. Since Patsy had looked at her leukemia as "rain," she had looked at the rainbow as a sign to her that God was in control of her life. Throughout her illness she believed the rainbow spoke to her, "God is in control."

I knew that although this circular rainbow could be explained scientifically, I received it as a sign from God that He was in control of the airplane, and I need not fear.

Then while reflecting on my rainbow miracle I dozed off. As we touched down in Perm, I woke up and was relieved the trip was safely over. When the jetliner came to a screeching halt, I sighed with a grin and thought, *We made it!* It was no surprise to me, however. After all, hadn't I had inside information that all would be well?

"Thank you, Jesus," I whispered.

25

Spiritually Overdosed

After arriving back home, I didn't want to think about my trip to Russia. I didn't want to pray, and I didn't want to read the Bible. What was wrong with me? I dreamed about the trip for a week after I returned, and I was sick of thinking about it. But why? I couldn't understand it. We had experienced a glorious trip with almost 5,000 receiving Christ as Savior and Lord. God had blessed me immeasurably, but it was always like this after a mission trip. I wanted to forget about it. It was almost as if I needed some space or needed to take a deep breath. It reminded me of claustrophobia.

Because I didn't want to pray or read the Bible, guilt overwhelmed me. Joe irritated me, and I had a critical attitude. It seemed that after a mountaintop experience like Russia, I'd act more Christlike, but the opposite proved true.

My second week home, nightmares started, and I couldn't sleep at night. At least my dreams of the trip had stopped after I had asked God to stop them. But now I would wake up in the middle of the night and couldn't go back to sleep. We were told we might experience a reverse culture shock upon returning home. Was this what was happening?

I went to the Lord and asked Him to show me any sin in my life so I could repent. If I had a bad attitude I wanted to make it right. I wasn't aware of any grudges I might be holding but asked the Lord to show any to me. When no one came to mind, I determined the nightmares were harassment from the enemy. That night before I went to sleep, I asked the Lord to shield my mind from the enemy and give me sweet sleep. I slept soundly and woke up rested.

I asked the Lord to show me why I didn't want to read the Bible and pray. He didn't answer me, but instead the words came to my mind, "Do not pray or read the Bible for a week." What? *Surely*, I thought, *those were words from the devil.* God wouldn't tell me not to pray or read the Bible, would He? But I had been waiting on an answer from the Lord, and somehow I had to believe those words, as bizarre as they seemed, came from Him.

After thinking about it for a moment, I thought, *Okay, for one week I won't read the Bible or pray,* and immediately it was as though a big burden lifted off my shoulders. I was set free and began spontaneously to praise the Lord in song. I laughed because I hadn't wanted to pray, and yet, here I was, praising the Lord because I couldn't help myself.

I began to think about what had taken place and God showed me my problem. I had experienced a spiritual and emotional overdose in Russia, and my spirit needed a fast. It was as though, physically, I had eaten too much food, and my body needed a rest from food. So much had happened on our busy schedule in Russia that my mind also needed a break. I compared it to running ten miles without stopping. My body would then need to stop and recuperate. That's what my mind and spirit needed; to stop and recuperate.

Much of my prayer life was usually intercession—warfare. To think about warring in the spirit exhausted me, because I needed some R& R. Because I wasn't up to warfare, I felt guilty. Even though I knew where the guilt came from, I still thought I should pray. But I had been on the front lines, and now it was time to fall back and rest. This sounded strange to me, especially coming from God, and I had never heard anything like it before, but I trusted His guidance, and knew it wouldn't put an end to me even if it weren't from Him. The release in my spirit was glorious, and the guilt left.

The next morning I awoke with a praise song in my heart, and I arose to give my house a thorough cleaning. I started with the bathroom and cleaned out every drawer and scrubbed the cabinets. I listened to my favorite Christian radio station as I worked, and as I cleaned I realized my mind was resting.

Not reading the Word proved to be more difficult the next day. I usually read Psalms and Proverbs every day along with a couple of chapters from the Old and New Testaments, and I especially missed reading Psalms. I started to pick up my Bible, but felt a check in my spirit. This was certainly a unique experience. I missed my Psalms, as it had always been like medicine to me, but I resisted reading.

The following day, fasting from the Word was even more difficult. I found myself talking to the Lord throughout the day, mostly praise, when I least expected it. It was not burdensome, as if I was simply conversing with a friend. It was almost impossible not to talk to Him spontaneously, and I didn't even realize I was doing it. I wasn't praying intentionally. It just happened. Was this what "Pray without ceasing"[23] meant?

Each day I got hungrier and hungrier for the Word. It reminded me of being on a diet and wanting chocolate. How I loved my chocolate. It was so difficult to resist chocolate when I craved it. That's how I felt about God's Word. It was as though I craved it.

After the fact, I thought it was interesting because God knew all the time how I would react to the fast from His Word or prayer. By not reading the Bible, I realized how much I wanted and needed it. As far back as I could remember, I had not gone a week without reading it. I could hardly wait until my week was up.

I assumed it was okay to read the Bible in church and Sunday school in line with this experiment. I believe He knew I couldn't get rid of the guilt so He had to tell me not to pray or read the Bible. I did read it during the teaching at Sunday school and during the sermon, but that was the only time.

As I continued to clean my house, my mind became more and more rested. I thought how I was God's clay to be molded as He wished. He knew what was best for me.

How unspiritual this fast seemed to the mind of a Christian. But God knew I desired to serve Him with all my heart. Wasn't that why I had gone to Russia in the first place? He released me from the guilt of the law—what we "ought to do," and by doing so, I became hungry for His Word and could hardly not pray, as I was so used to talking to Him spontaneously.

I thought of the scripture "Neither are your ways my ways…"[24] and I thanked God that He was the potter and I was the clay. He always knew what was best for me, and all He required was obedience, even when it sounded strange. What a gentle, loving Father I served.

Russia (5), 1995

26

God Still Speaks Through Dreams

The following spring I began to think about my next trip to the former USSR. Trips to Latvia and Russia were scheduled that summer, and I wanted to go both places, but knew I couldn't. This would be my fifth trip to Russia. What to do?

Returning to the same church in Latvia would certainly be rewarding. I could renew friendships and see how the church had grown. In Russia we would be visiting different cities rather than returning to those where we had ministered before.

Monday morning in my quiet time I began to pray about where to go. I knew that, first of all, I had to get my strength back or I couldn't go anywhere. Presently my health was a chief concern. As I began to pray about the trip, emotionally I couldn't handle it. I wasn't up to the spiritual struggle I always had before each trip. There were still four months before the trip, so I didn't need to know immediately what God wanted me to do.

I placed the matter in God's hands, and asked Him to let me know what He wanted me to do in His own timing. I simply couldn't think about it at that moment, and as I prayed, the burden lifted. Peace came, and I knew I didn't have to think about it anymore. What I needed to do was concentrate on my health so I would be able to go.

I opened the Bible to Psalm 41 for my regular daily Bible reading. The verse, highlighted in yellow, read, "The Lord will help them when they are sick and will restore them to health." [25] The words seemed to leap off the page at me, and my heart pounded as though it might jump out of my chest. I knew this was God's promise that I would be physically able to make the trip.

Sobbing, I thanked Him over and over again for His precious guidance. After regaining some composure, I looked back at the Word and could hardly believe my eyes. In the margin beside the scripture I had written, "Russia #4, 6/9/94."

Whoa! It was like a double confirmation since it was the exact scripture the Lord had given me the summer before after a five-week siege of pneumonia to confirm that I would be able to make that trip. God used the same scripture two trips in a row to guarantee my health for the trips. I hadn't flipped through the pages to try to find that scripture. It was in my Bible reading for that very day. I continued to be amazed how God's Word spoke to me when I needed it on a certain day. I was relieved and felt renewed faith that my body would be completely healed.

That afternoon I wrote my column for the newspaper that had nothing to do with the mission trip. In it, however, I wrote, "I believe in dreams, for I've been directed in dreams. I've learned that dreams are sometimes God's way of getting through to us."

When I had been unwilling to travel to Brazil, God showed me in a dream that I was to go. Because I didn't want to accept His leading in my conscious state, He had gone to my subconscious and made His will known. After working through my feelings, I gladly went. Little did I know that in less than 24 hours my column on dreams would have added meaning.

That night I dreamed all night that I was on a mission trip to Latvia. I saw myself in hospital corridors and schools, completely frustrated, because I was not able to witness one-on-one. In the dream, as our team waited at the airport to fly home, I remarked sadly, "I didn't pray with one person to receive Christ."

I awoke, emotionally distraught. Because of my deep despondency in the dream, I knew this was God's way of telling me I was to travel to Russia that summer, not Latvia.

I remembered what I'd written in my article the day before. "I believe in dreams, for I've been directed in dreams. I've learned that sometimes that's God's way of getting through to us." It was almost as though I had prophetically penned those words so they would come back and reassure me that God had spoken.

The timing of all this was incredible. Within 24 hours God had affirmed I would be in good health for the trip, and He had shown me I was to go to Russia. I had not struggled over it, but God, in His gentle, loving way, had brought it to me. It taught me that I, sometimes, fretted too much in an attempt to hear God. I just needed to leave my problems with Him, and He would work them out for me in His own way and in His own time.

27

Triumphing over Difficulties

When the mission team from our church arrived at the airport, an agent told Mary Nan Foster and me the airline was overbooked and there weren't any seats available for us. I knew God was up to something, so I imagined that we'd be seated in the first-class section. Shortly, however, two people volunteered to go on a later flight, so, fortunately, we were able to go with our group. Not only did Mary Nan and I get seats, we got them together.

We expected 58 members of our larger team to arrive from Amarillo but were informed their plane was going to be late. The airline agent regretfully told us she didn't think our plane could be held for them. So our team got together and prayed that God would, somehow, hold that plane. After we boarded the plane, the pilot announced, "Due to a scratch on the plane, there will be a slight delay, so it can be checked out."

We almost shouted. "Sure!" I smugly muttered in between laughs. A scratch, for sure. Our team knew better, and if there really was a scratch, we figured an angel had put it there. The Amarillo team finally arrived, and one hour later we lifted off.

On our first day of witnessing in Moscow we rode the bus to Red Square. The tour guide told us that St. Basil, Russia's most famous cathedral, and located on Red Square, was built by Ivan the Terrible. He had a tower chapel built for each war victory. The towers comprised

St. Basil. After the chapel was completed, Ivan blinded the master artist who had created it, so he could never again recreate anything so elaborate. The tour guide told us that although the outside is beautiful, the inside, where visitors are not allowed, is plain and ugly.

The first day we had to walk a long way before we got to the bus, and my ankles swelled up badly, but I was determined that wasn't going to stop me from ministering. That night after church I asked Oleg (the host in the home where we stayed) if he would call a taxi for me, which he did. There was no way I could walk back to the house. My ankles gave me problems throughout the week as we walked door to door witnessing. I didn't go witnessing one afternoon, because I could hardly walk. The previous day we had walked more than usual, from morning until 10:00 p.m. without stopping.

I thought, *I can't think of a better way to make one's feet swell than witnessing for Jesus.* When I thought of what Jesus took for me on His walk to Calvary, my swollen ankles were nothing compared to what He had endured. One evening my feet were hurting so badly that we quit walking door to door. To multiply our time, instead of us women going to church at night, when the men preached, we continued to witness in homes. Because of my ankle problem that night, however, we chose to go to church. Dennis Rumbo was having problems with one of his feet, so we asked the church to pray for us. The next day my ankles felt strong and ready to go. How grateful I was for the power in prayer and for a God who answered.

What a unique, delightful experience it was, staying in the home of nationals. The Russians spoke no English, and about all we could say in Russian was *"Spaciba,"* which means, "Thank you." So we made hand gestures all week to communicate.

One morning we sat down to breakfast where we were served raw bacon with our eggs. What to do? We didn't want to embarrass our hostess, so with a smile, I pointed to the bacon and then to the stove. She got the picture and cooked it for us. We learned that all foods in Russia are served at any meal. One morning for breakfast we were served spaghetti with weiners, cucumbers, tomatoes, and pickles. One evening we had eggs. For us Texans our hostess cooked chicken fried steak almost every other day, or a similar version of it, that tasted delicious. IC had prepaid the host for our meals, the payment coming from team members' expense for the trip. The host was also given suggestions for our meals. They outdid themselves trying to please us in every way, and in spite of a week with no verbal communication, we came away feeling much love for these precious people.

The main stumbling block of witnessing to the Russians was their economic conditions. They didn't believe God loved them. One woman told me that it was too late for Russia to know God. After I explained that knowing Christ was an individual decision for each person and that it is never too late, she readily prayed to receive Christ.

My interpreter, Yelena, a member of the Russian Orthodox Church, had not understood that being a believer meant a personal relationship with God. One day I asked her if she had ever prayed the prayer of repentance. She answered, laughing, "Yes, I've prayed it every time I've interpreted it for you these last three days." Seeing our helpers come to know God was one of our greatest joys on the crusades.

When I had explained the way to God through Jesus Christ to one atheist, he said, "We were not taught that way. I don't believe in God." Often in dealing with an atheist, words fell on deaf ears, but this time words that I had not even considered before, came quickly to my mind.

I told him about visiting the Armory Museum at the Kremlin where I had seen crosses on gold-gilded carriages, crowns, and thrones. I reminded him that God once had been an important part of Russia and probably his grandparents or great-grandparents had known God. This seemed to get his attention as he nodded in agreement.

I told him that America had learned of God because people from Europe brought this good news to us, and now that Russia had opened up again, we wanted to bring God's truth back to them. We had heard their leaders taught them there was no God, but we knew there was a God because we knew Him personally.

I challenged him that sometimes in life we are taught wrong precepts, and once we are faced with the truth, we must make a decision either to continue to believe an error or to accept the truth. I read the Bible to him where Jesus says, "I am the way, and the truth, and the life.

No one comes to the Father but through Me."[26] My eyes filled with tears as I explained we had come a long way to tell him the truth because we cared. I then told him we didn't want him to trust Jesus for us, but for himself so that he would know the Lord and have the peace and joy that we did. I didn't want him to say, "Yes," just to appease me.

But when I went over the questions again with him, he prayed to receive Christ. I was ecstatic. I believe many atheists are not so much in defiance of God as they are ignorant of the truth. The young people up to the age of about 40 were more receptive of the salvation message than the older generation, which had been steeped in communism.

The June 14, 1995, edition of the *Moscow Times* read, "Yeltsin spoke of the evils of the communist regime which the collapse of the Soviet Union effectively destroyed. He spoke of the destruction of one of the worst, most merciless totalitarian systems."

Because of economic conditions, many Russians would welcome back the communist rule. They saw organized crime increase as they watched civil servants abandon their duties in the frenzied desire to make money.

Because the Russians kept their houses so warm, I got sick on Tuesday. I rested Wednesday, but determined there wasn't time to waste being sick, so I trusted the Lord for my well-being, one meeting at a time.

Friday we went to a home visit, then to a children's art class in a government building to take cartoon New Testaments. By this time I was beginning to feel pretty stretched out, with a headache, congestion and weakness. Much to my dismay I learned that Mary Nan and I were scheduled to go to another home. All I wanted to do was go back to the hotel and sleep. I was feeling very much "in the flesh," and in no way was I up to witnessing.

There was no way I could play the disco and share my testimony, because I felt so ill, so I told Mary Nan she would need to do it.

"Let's wait and see how the Holy Spirit leads," she answered.

She doesn't want to do it, either, I thought, but I said nothing. I was sure the Holy Spirit would lead her to do the witnessing.

When we arrived at the home, the hostess said they had been up since 4:00 a.m. preparing a meal for 20 people. We sat down at the table, and Mary Nan and I introduced ourselves. We told a little about our families, and when I told them of my eight grandchildren, they "ooooohed" and "aaaaahed" and clapped. I laughed since they were applauding me for something with which I had nothing to do.

When I told them we came to share the love of Jesus, suddenly the Holy Spirit came upon me and filled me with so great a love for these people, that more than anything in the world, I wanted to share with them the good news of Jesus Christ. God had literally transformed my attitude, filled me with strength, and I thought I would burst if I didn't share with them. Hoping with all my heart that Mary Nan wouldn't mind, I told her, "I think I'm supposed to share tonight."

"I know you are. God revealed it to me, and I've already been praying for you," she answered as she laughed. How grateful I was for a praying partner. If I ever needed prayer, it was then.

Some of the people asked such simple questions, like why Jesus had to come to die in the first place. I explained about Adam and Eve and the fall of man as simply as I could, and it was as though a light came on in their eyes. When we answered other questions with scriptures, they readily accepted.

I thought of Paul in the Bible saying our weakness was made strong in the Lord. God was certainly sustaining me. I wasn't tired anymore, my headache was gone, and my congestion had cleared up. I was amazed.

Three of the women shed tears before we got halfway through the questionnaire. Most of the questions they asked, any six-year-old child active in Sunday school here at home could have answered. Two women had read ahead of us and had filled out the whole questionnaire and were ready to pray.

Nine prayed to receive Christ, and five of those were in the same family as the hostess, who was a member of our host church. Everyone was so happy. They had been like hungry children longing for just the right answers. When their questions were answered, and they understood , they readily prayed to receive Christ.

From my journal on the train to Moscow after the crusade: "I'm really tired today with fever blisters all over my mouth, and I miss Joe so much. I started the day with swollen ankles, so my feet and legs hurt so much that at bedtime I can't sleep. All I can think of is seeing Joe, and I cry every time I think of him. I am SO homesick! I'm ready to see my 'honey' and home!

"This trip has truly been a miracle, physically, for me. I'm amazed that less than two months ago I panted after walking from the car to the house at home. Cyndi (my daughter) was so scared I couldn't make this trip. Now I've walked so many miles, probably five miles one day, and it never bothered my lungs, only my feet and legs. God promised I would have health for the trip, and, in spite of my ankle problems, I did. I'm going home feeling much stronger than when I came."

The trip proved successful, with almost 10,000 salvations reported for the whole crusade. Although I had witnessed the presence and leading of the Holy Spirit on other trips, this experience stands out as the one I remember most to see that truly we are but vessels as God does His work through us.

As I look on, a little girl is all smiles after she prayed to receive Christ.

Russia (6), 1997

28

"Yes, Lord"

The Lord impressed upon me the following year that I was not to go on a mission trip. I had thought, perhaps, I might not ever go on a trip again. But the next year, in early 1997, I began to sense in my spirit that I would again be traveling soon. I believed that God had given me plenty of time to recuperate from illnesses.

I had become burdened about China, so thought I probably would go back to the Orient again if I went anywhere. So many believers had ministered in Russia since Glasnost had opened up the former Soviet Union, but China was still under Communist rule.

As time passed, the idea of a trip became stronger and stronger in my mind. Then for about a week when I would hear anything on the news about Russia, my heart would leap. I was so sure that I would be going to China that I wondered what was going on. One day I heard China mentioned on TV news, but it didn't phase me. I wondered if God was drawing me back to Russia. I fought against the idea, because I didn't want to go back to Russia. I figured five trips was enough. The country was dreary and gray, and it rained a lot. No, I did not want to go back to Russia.

I couldn't get away from the feeling, however, that I was being led to Russia. One morning at church a deacon testified about missing God's purpose because of disobedience. He spoke right to my heart, because I suspected I was fighting the idea of going to Russia.

Then a woman gave testimony about obedience and all I remembered that she said was, "Just do it!" My heart pounded, and I knew God was speaking to me, "Just go to Russia."

On the way home from church I told Joe that God was dealing with me about Russia, and I asked him to pray with me about it.

That afternoon I curled up on the couch to finish reading a book, while all the time thoughts of Russia bombarded me. Finally I told the Lord I would go, but my heart had been set on going with someone who believed in praying for the sick.

As I pondered on it the Lord spoke in my spirit, "I know you want to pray for the sick, but I'm coming soon, and we must get the family in. Evangelism is where I need you right now." I knew He meant the family of God. I hadn't expected that. I knew God must be speaking, because since that wasn't what I wanted to hear, I certainly wouldn't have come up with the idea myself. I was disappointed, but more than anything I wanted to be in His will.

Since evangelism was the full thrust of this trip, I decided to go with International Crusades, again, because their method of witnessing is so successful.

I needed a sure-fire confirmation, however, to make sure all these things weren't a figment of my imagination. Talk about a slow learner! I quickly learned that God was up to any challenge. I was still reading my book when these words dropped into my mind, "Call Nancy Corley and invite her to go to Russia. If she'll go, that is your confirmation."

I dropped the book and sat, stunned. Where did those words come from? Surely I didn't make them up. I had never considered asking Nancy, because I knew she was considering a Jamaican mission trip. She had said she wasn't going back to Russia either. I finally accepted the thought as being from God. The only thing to do was call Nancy and invite her to go to Russia. I thought, *She probably will think I'm crazy, but I've got to call her just the same.* If the words hadn't been from God, we'd both have a good laugh over it. So I dialed Nancy's number.

"Hello, Nancy," I said. "This is a strange call." I paused, my heart throbbing, "But has God been dealing with you about going back to Russia?"

Dead silence filled the air before she slowly asked, "How...did... you...know?" Nancy then said God had been dealing with her, as thoughts of Russia and the good times we'd had there had been coming to her mind. She, too, had wondered if God was drawing her back to Russia.

When I told her of my "words from God," she readily agreed to the trip. "Your phone call is my confirmation," she said.

I thought, *It is certainly mine!*

I wanted to shout and run through the house and jump up and down. What I was most excited about was that I had literally heard from God. It was so wonderful being a Christian, and hearing God was the best blessing of all.

Once I knew for sure the trip to Russia was God's will, I was ready to pack. The country's dreariness didn't matter anymore, only the souls that would be saved. Again and again I thanked God for allowing me another opportunity to witness in Russia.

I happened to remember that several others from our church were going to the Ukraine almost the same time we would be in Russia. Jim Walters was leading that group, and since we had served together on several trips, I would much prefer to go with his team.

Also the weather would be nicer since the Ukraine was further south, and the oppression wasn't nearly so heavy there as in Russia. Jim's team would fly to the Ukraine from Moscow, whereas the Russia team would have to ride a hot, noisy, overnight train to our region.

Wouldn't Nancy and I be able to help the Ukraine team of four since none of them had been on a mission trip before? Joe even agreed that it would make more sense to go with them.

But peace wouldn't come. Russia seemed to pop out in my mind over and over. But why? I could lead just as many souls to the Lord in the Ukraine as in Russia. Why did it matter?

While babysitting at my daughter's home I lay back in a chaise lounge reading and praying—arguing with God. The words came to my mind, "What are your motives for wanting to go to the Ukraine?" After considering the question, I had to admit they were mostly for the wrong reasons. The bottom line was I didn't want to go to Russia again.

"I have designed a special plan for you in Russia," came words, gentle but stern.

"Okay, Lord, whatever you want," I said. How thankful I was for a patient God.

A few days later, during my quiet time, I picked up a Russia brochure to read over our daily schedule, which I hadn't done before. To my astonishment, we would be stopping over at London. My grandfather had immigrated from England when he was nine months old, and I had wanted to go to London for years. This would be a dream come true for me.

I couldn't believe my eyes as I read on. On our return trip from Russia, we would SPEND THE NIGHT in London. My mind reeled. I would fill up on coffee and stay up all night, sightseeing. Ecstatic, I ran to the telephone to call Nancy Corley to see if she'd read about London. She had, and by the end of our conversation we had made plans to stay over in London a few extra days on our return trip home.

Then I told her about my Ukranian battle with the Lord, and how God had not let me see the part about London in our brochure until I was willing to do it His way. Otherwise, I probably would've let London sway my decision and gone to Russia for the wrong reason. This story was getting better and better.

As the wheels began to turn I remembered my friend, Jacque Heasley, had stayed in London with some church members there as she went back and forth to Africa on mission trips. So I called her to see what the possibilities were for Nancy and me to do the same. She agreed to contact the church in London and see what she could do.

Was a few days in London part of God's plan for me? I didn't know, but I felt God was up to something, and I knew it would be good. Anxiously, I waited to hear from Jacque. Was my dream about to be fulfilled?

Finally the long awaited call came. "It's all set," Jacque announced.

As it turned out, on our way home from Russia, the London church put Nancy and me up for three nights in the home of a lovely family who couldn't have been more gracious. We saw the sights of England by tour, by bus, by trolley, and by train, but mostly by the grace of God.

Someday maybe I'd learn to say, "Yes, Lord," without arguing.

29

Christian Persecution Increases in Russia

On this trip our three-person team served in Shigri, a city of 35,000, whose churches included only one Orthodox church and one Baptist church of 60 members that met in a cinema. The Orthodox church certainly did not want us there, and the Baptist church didn't trust us. The fact that I had already served in five other Russian cities did not matter to them.

Although there was a time after Glasnost when evangelists could witness freely in Russia, that was no longer the case. Oppression and persecution of the evangelical church in Russia was growing rapidly. The Russian Orthodox Church was threatened by missionaries coming to their country, and although the evangelical churches were feeling the crunch, they continued on.

Perm, the city where we held a crusade in 1994, had closed to Western religions two years later. Ben Mieth, our International Crusades team leader, reminded us that a successful witness was sharing Christ in the power of the Holy Spirit, then leaving the results to God. He also reminded us that God was the Lord of the harvest, and we were but servants here to tell the good news. Then he said, "Mountaintop experiences are wonderful, but most of the work has to be done in the valley."

His words hit home when we learned *The Ostrogozhsk* newspaper ran an advertisement paid for by the Russian Orthodox Church to warn people of our coming evangelistic crusade. It read that Americans were coming to ask them questions and would take their answers back to their government, which, of course, was not true.

In June, 1997, the Department of Religion in Russia declared that only four religions would be allowed in Russia: Christian (represented by the Russian Orthodox Church,) Islam, Hinduism, and Buddhism.

That same month, the Department of Religion announced that only churches 15 years or older could remain open. This would exclude many evangelical churches organized since Glasnost began in 1989, which was exactly what the Russian Orthodox wanted. The up side to this was the law excluded the many cults which had invaded the former USSR.

Although many citizens were atheists, many others were hungry for God's Word. In the marketplace an elderly woman discovered our mission and literally ran up to a team member and shouted, "You must tell everybody! You must tell everybody!"

One day we ate lunch at McDonald's Hamburgers, when two boys about 12 years old who were in line ahead of us, heard us talking. They began to snicker and look at us, so I gave each of them my testimony, which they read carefully, and then marked each question "Yes." One boy kept looking over the shoulder of the other one, copying what he had checked. The first boy read slowly and carefully the prayer for salvation before he marked "Yes." We finished the questions just as the boys got to the front of the line to place their order. I believed the young man who was serious about the questionnaire truly prayed to receive the Lord.

This trip proved to be my most trying one yet. First, the host church was unprepared for our method of witnessing. Its mission pastor, who traveled from an hour away in Kursk to Shigri only on Sundays, had been unable to attend preparation meetings for the crusade. Therefore the church leaders were totally ignorant of our methods, feared our evangelistic questionnaire and didn't think the Russian people would accept it. They, too, had heard we would take the questionnaires back to our government. The Russian Orthodox Church tried to keep us from meeting, and Ivan, one of the preachers from our church, spent all afternoon at the city office trying to get permission for us to meet and witness on the street.

Ivan said the people were afraid to sign their names for fear of aggression, and he didn't want us to ask them to sign the questionnaires anymore. City hall said we had to have a special paper from America saying we could hold the meetings. Our team was stopped on the streets of Shigri by a policeman who checked our credentials. Then policemen parked their jeep on the street near our flat. I was not afraid for ourselves, but was concerned that they wouldn't let us witness. My concerns proved to be true when the mayor of Shigri denied our rights to witness on the streets or to hold services.

After the mayor's declaration, Ivan drove to Kursk to obtain a special document from the area bishop who gave us permission to continue our crusade without interference from the city government. That night two policemen were in the service to investigate. We later learned the Department of Religion had warned people they would lose their jobs if they came to the services at the cinema.

Ivan read Acts 4:18-20 to our team. "So they called the apostles back in and told them never again to speak or teach about Jesus. But Peter and John replied, 'Do you think God wants us to obey you rather than him? We cannot stop telling about the wonderful things we have seen and heard.'"[27] It felt as though we were living the Bible itself. Even though streets were not the safest place to be, we went anyway, because homes were not opened to us.

To make matters worse, the only translator that could be found in Shigri was an English teacher, Svetlana, who was proud of being an atheist. She had no intention of cooperating with us but was our only means of communication with the people for three days. She tried to turn our local church members against us. She did not translate well and insisted that Bill Young, our team leader, write down his sermon, word for word, for her. We tried to explain the difficulty in this because the Holy Spirit often leads a speaker down a path much different from the written script, but it went right over her head, because she didn't understand anything about the Holy Spirit.

She called our church "an organization with a program." Nadia, another atheist translator and a teacher friend of Svetlana's, came to help, and neither Nadia nor Svetlana wanted us to use the questionnaires and tried to talk us out of using them.

There was heavy friction between the translators and our team. I asked Svetlana over and over to first read the testimony, as it laid the groundwork for the questions, before having them fill out the questionnaire, but she'd continue to avoid the testimony and go straight to the questions. I was determined two atheists were not going to deter our mission of winning souls.

Luda, a teenage girl from church, who spoke no English, went with us as we attempted to witness on the streets. She learned how to witness by watching us, and in spite of the translators, she prayed with many to receive Christ. She did so well we didn't even need the translators, so Bill, our team leader, paid Svetlana and Nadia and dismissed them.

Ben Mieth, who was leading a team in Kursk, learned of our situation and sent us his own translator, who was already trained in our method of witnessing, spoke perfect English and was blessed with a servant's heart. What a relief. Our cloud of frustration lifted, and the crusade proceeded as planned.

That evening Ivan poured out his heart to our team concerning problems in the church. Ivan felt that if a person didn't come to church for a year, he should be excluded from the congregation. He also wanted to be the judge of whether or not a person was born again. Ivan also had problems with his pastor because the two of them didn't agree on biblical beliefs, and Ivan was concerned that the church might split because of it. He thought everyone should be on fire for the Lord like he was. Speaking to him metaphorically, I said not everyone was like the Apostle Paul. There were also Andrew and Thomas. I agreed it would be wonderful if everyone was like the Apostle Paul, but that that just was not the case. He wasn't too happy about my answer, but didn't have an argument. We found that Russians were by and large legalistic, and emphasis on "works" brought about a judgmental attitude.

I woke up the next morning with scriptures on my mind about spiritual authority. I thought they were for Ivan, but as the day wore on,

I realized God wanted me to share the scriptures that night at church. I did not want to, but Nancy Corley and Bill both encouraged me to do it if God was leading. There was no doubt about God's leading, and when I got my message written down on paper, I found it easy to deliver.

I read several scriptures about spiritual authority, then shared my testimony about how, when God showed Joe and me insight into His Word, we realized we needed to change churches, because we didn't believe like our present church anymore. We did not want to cause a problem in our present church because of our new beliefs, so we met with our pastor and told him of our decision. It was not an easy decision since we had been members of that church for almost 20 years, but we knew it had to be done.

I prayed that Ivan would get the message, but also hoped he wouldn't think my testimony was aimed at him. Later, Ivan thanked me for saying what I did and said it helped him tremendously. I was so relieved.

Back at our home-away-from-home, Bill asked what I thought of women preachers. I told him I believed men are to lead, but if they don't, then women should, because God's work has to go on. I told him, "Men preach. Women share." Then laughing, I added, "If you'll let me proclaim my Jesus, you can call it whatever you want."

Nancy and I shared with Bill how God had worked in our lives to bring us to Russia.

"You need to put those stories in a book," Bill encouraged. "It would really help new Christians understand the reality of God."

"Maybe I will, someday," I answered, newly inspired.

Our host church in Russia had been the focus of religious persecution between the 1940s and the 1960s. Nine of its members went to prison for their faith and some died there. One man served ten years and upon time for his release, was asked if he would continue to preach Jesus. When he answered in the affirmative, he was sentenced to seven more years in prison.

During this time believers met secretly in barns and cellars and baptized at night. Our host church was without a pastor for ten years, during which time a woman led the church. The men were in prison for their faith. Still a member, she now served as church historian. She said the Holy Spirit even told them, individually, where to meet from week to week so they wouldn't be caught by the KGB. Most of the time they met at different places in the woods.

The economy worsened as teachers, doctors, nurses, engineers and others paid by the government did not receive compensation for months that year. I asked the woman in whose home we stayed why she continued to teach school when she was not getting paid. Her eyes rolled upward as if to say, "What a stupid question," but she answered, "The children have to learn." I was touched by her commitment.

As we visited the home of Ivan, he asked us to pray for his mother-in-law who was very ill and could not speak. At 80 years old she was ready to transfer to her heavenly home, and they asked me to pray that she would get well or that God would take her home quickly. Although I was hesitant, because they had requested it with such fervor, I prayed.

We got word the following day, much to my surprise, that the little woman had died, and her family credited me with her death. They thanked me over and over for my prayer. I had mixed emotions about it, but was glad they were pleased, and knew it was a blessing the little grandmother was out of her misery.

And they say prayer doesn't work! I thought. This had certainly been a first for me. I never before prayed for someone to die. I could imagine my jovial family's response when they heard of this answered prayer.

"First you pray for God to supply your finances for Peru and somebody breaks his leg. Now you pray for someone to die, and they do. What are you going to pray for next?"

I thought, *One thing for sure is, walking with the Lord is a constant surprise. You never know what might happen next.*

Although the times were changing in Russia, it was sometimes difficult to tell whether the changes were good or bad. One nationalist stated, "At Glasnost there was plenty of money, but no goods. Now there are plenty of goods, but no money to buy them."

In spite of our problems, by the end of the week, church leaders had totally accepted us.

We had become "family," and we saw 80 people pray to receive Christ in Shigri.

Looking at cartoon Bibles with Russian boys at their school.

Zimbabwe, 2000

30

Overcoming Fears Abroad

With my eyes closed during praise and worship one Sunday morning in church, suddenly, the words "Go to Africa" dropped into my mind. As had happened so many times before, it was as though someone spoke to me audibly, but I knew better. Shocked, I opened my eyes and thought, *Now where did those words come from?* I hadn't been thinking about Africa, or any other place for that matter.

Another time God had spoken to me about going to Africa. He had even given me a vision of a sea of shaved black heads with big oval holes for eyes that looked empty and hopeless. I didn't know then that African people shaved their heads.

Was this God speaking to me to go to Africa? I thought so, and checked with International Commission (formerly International Crusades) to see when their next trip to Africa was scheduled, but it was in November when I would be teaching school. Perhaps, God was preparing me for a future trip.

The following spring, as I was getting ready for church one Sunday morning, a radio deejay was speaking to college students. "What are you going to do for God this summer?" His question spoke right to my heart. I immediately thought of Africa, but we had four events already scheduled for my summer vacation, and I didn't see how anything else would fit in. So I dismissed the thought for the time being. After a few days of wrestling with the idea, I reminded the Lord that we had a pretty full summer, but if a trip to Africa fit in with our schedule, I would take that as my confirmation to go. When I checked the schedule, I was amazed when the trip to Zimbabwe fit like the final piece of a puzzle.

Traveling to Africa would be a real milestone for me, because this would be the fifth continent on which I would proclaim the gospel of Jesus Christ.

On most of my trips I had felt no fear, either before going or while away, but this trip would prove to be different. The more I heard about the AIDS epidemic in Africa and the political problems with the black people murdering white farmers and taking over their farms, the more fearful I became. Black nationals had murdered 38 white farmers. What if a black national decided that since I was white I, too, must die? People did crazy things these days.

I was also afraid that, somehow, I might get the horrible, dreaded AIDS disease. I had read that 50 percent of the 15-year-old boys living in Africa then would die of AIDS. Although I wanted to go to Africa, these seemingly insurmountable problems overcame my desires to go. Finally, I told the Lord I'd be willing to go, but if He didn't want me to go, I would be just as happy for Him to close the doors for me.

I called IC and they assured me we would be working in the city of Gweru and would not be in the country on any farms. As always they would not allow us to go any place where we might be in danger. My concerns about the white farmers subsided. One day while praying the words from Psalm 91:7 jumped off the page at me: "Though a thousand fall at your side, though ten thousand are dying around you, these evils will not touch you."[28] God was speaking to me about AIDS. I knew it. His promise of safety brought added peace.

The following Sunday Bro. Bob's sermon's title was, *Here am I, Send Me.* I had to laugh. How more direct could God be?

God, you had him preach that sermon just for me, didn't you? I thought. I knew then that I would be on that plane to Zimbabwe. After the church service I went to the altar to tell Bro. Bob and the church family that I was going to Zimbabwe. From then on there was no more doubt—or fear. Peace was mine, and I was Africa bound.

I typed up Psalm 91, the "Protection Psalm," with my name in every phrase that was applicable, gave a copy to my church, family, and friends and asked them to pray it over me each day I was in Africa. I would heavily rely on God to answer their prayers to get me through the trip.

31

A Tough Start

Two days before we were to leave I realized the printed personal testimony/questionnaires that we used in witnessing had not arrived. Nor had I received my plane ticket. When I called IC they were surprised and said I should have already received both, until they discovered I wasn't even on the list to go, because I had not sent in enough money for my ticket. I was waiting until the last minute to get all my money in, in case I received any more in the mail. I quickly got my money in, and IC said they'd have Reyburn Ruhl meet me at the airport to bring me my ticket and testimonies. I was on my way!

Most of the team would be coming from California, and we would all meet up at Atlanta, so I was to meet only two other team members, Stacey Ford and Kristy Garza, at D/FW Airport. We were scheduled to leave at 5:30 p.m. After I received my ticket and testimonies from Reyburn, we all chatted and got to know one another as we whiled away the time waiting to board the plane.

Finally, a voice sounded over the speaker that it was time to board so Reyburn bid us farewell. Stacey and Kristy went ahead of me, and when I handed the agent my ticket, his words sent me into shock.

"I'm sorry, ma'am. This flight left 30 minutes ago. You cannot board this plane."

Speechless and horrified, I managed, "But I'm going with a group to Africa. I HAVE to get on this plane." I looked at my ticket, and sure enough, it was for the 5:00 flight. I looked around for Reyburn, but he was nowhere in sight. So there I stood, alone, with no one to verify the travel agent had made a mistake.

"Sorry, ma'am. You can try 'standby' right over there," he said as he pointed.

I couldn't believe it. There was no way I could make this trip alone.

I rushed over to standby where there were already two long lines. I didn't have time to stand in line. I had to get on that plane right now. A man in a uniform walked by and apparently could tell by my distressed look that I was in trouble big time. When he asked if he could help me, I frantically blurted out my problem, and he said he'd see what he could do.

I prayed. Oh, how I prayed. I didn't have time to worry. I was already stressed to the limit. Then I remembered a new praise song we had learned at church. All I could remember was the title, *"You are in control. You are in control. You are in control. You are in control."*[29] I leaned on the wall by the standby booth and sang it quietly over and over, trying to convince myself that God truly was in control. I knew God had called me to go to Zimbabwe. The finances had come in and I knew they wouldn't have, if God had not intended me to go.

Old Slewfoot certainly didn't want me to go on this trip. He seemed to be working overtime to keep me from going, but I was determined that, with God, I would have the victory. These trials simply meant this trip was going to be extra special. I waited and wondered what took the agent so long to return. I continued to pray and sing softly. If I kept my thoughts totally on Jesus, I had peace. If I started to think about any possibility of not getting on the plane, my nerves went berserk. So I sang and prayed, trusting God to work this out with every ounce of faith I had.

Finally, the agent returned. He took my elbow and quickly escorted me to the entrance gate while he handed me a boarding pass. I looked back to see the long lines still there at standby.

"Your ticket to Harrare has not been confirmed in Atlanta, and you must take care of that as soon as you arrive in Atlanta," he told me.

I nodded and thanked him for his help, and overcome with emotion, fought back tears as I scurried down the ramp. At least I had a seat on this plane. I would take one step at a time, trusting God to work out every detail of this trip. He hadn't failed me yet.

As I stepped through the door to the airplane, the airline attendant kindly informed me, "I'm sorry, but you'll have to check your carry-on, because all the overhead compartments are full."

God, this can't be happening! I thought. All my necessities were in that bag: my Bible, two cameras, medicine, cosmetics, hairdryer, and most of all, the testimony/questionnaires I would use in witnessing. I had reached my breaking point. Enough was enough. I wanted to sit down in the floor and have myself a good cry. Why had everything been so difficult for me? *What else is going to happen?* I wondered.

"Ma'am, I'm going to Africa, and there is no way to lock this carry-on. Is there not some way I can keep it with me?" I pleaded. She must have seen the desperation in my eyes.

"Just bring it on, and place it under the seat in front of you," she answered.

Tracey and Kristy waved at me with big smiles as I started down the aisle to my seat. I knew they'd been praying, too. As I collapsed into my seat, I was reminded of the song while waiting at the standby counter, only I changed the words to, *"You WERE in control! You WERE in control! You WERE in control! You WERE in control!"*

"Thank you, Lord! Thank you, Lord. Thank you, Lord," I prayed.

I met all the team in Atlanta and quickly went to get everything confirmed with the ticket agent, when to my anguish, there was more bad news on the way. Would it never stop?

"I'm sorry, ma'am, but your ticket has not been confirmed, and there are no seats available on this flight."

I was beginning to wonder if God really did want me to go to Africa, but, again, I was reminded He had paid my way.

The agent said that not only was I not confirmed at Atlanta but my ticket home from Harrare, Zimbabwe, had not been confirmed either. I thought, *Oh, great! They're going to get me to Africa and then leave me there!* But Mike Russell, our mission team leader, told me that airlines didn't confirm tickets in Africa like we did in the States and that no one's return ticket was confirmed yet.

Mike explained the situation to the airline agent, and the airline offered $500 to anyone who would go on a later flight. Fortunately, someone came forward to give me his seat. God had come through once again.

As we boarded the jetliner, I thought, *This is going to be some trip. I just know it! Zimbabwe, here we come!*

32

A White Farmer's Plantation

Our team worked out of ten churches in Gweru, but what IC didn't know was that one of the churches had two missions in the country. I was assigned to Senga Baptist Church, but the pastor wanted Clayton Jones and me to go to their mission at White Water Church which had not been listed on the agenda. They said it was about 20 minutes from Gweru, but it turned out to be closer to an hour. When I heard it was a plantation, my mind went into high gear, wondering if it might be a white farmer's plantation.

When I got into the truck to go to the plantation, the driver said, "You must pray for the tires. They are very thin. Do you have a flashlight?"

"Yes, I do," I answered, "why?"

"In case we have a flat," he answered. Did I ever start to pray!

We drove and drove before turning off the main highway onto a smaller one-lane road with pavement broken in places to the middle of the road. Talk about bumpy! Off of that road we turned onto a street that was very ridged, and the driver went unreasonably fast. The car went bumpety, bump over each ridge, one after another. *Why doesn't he slow down?* I thought. *No wonder his tires are shot!*

Finally we turned onto a dirt road, and as we entered what looked like a camp, I saw cows in several pens. "Maize corn," as they called it, was stacked in mounds all over the place at least ten feet high.

As we drove, thatched-roof huts as well as concrete houses with tin roofs slowly came into view. No one knew we were coming, but one woman we met told us she'd try to organize a meeting. We waited for an hour and walked about the camp where we learned that 50 families lived there and the plantation was owned by Ben Harrye.

Usually the meetings were held outside but because it was winter, we met inside a clinic that measured about 10 feet by 12 feet. I measured it by walking it off and comparing it to our dog pen at home.

When people began arriving, men brought their chairs while women brought a big straw mat for themselves and their children. In all we had about 30 people attending. As we sang praises to God a truck drove up, and a man stuck his head inside the clinic. He was white. My heart sank. This WAS one of those plantations where white farmers were getting murdered. Although, at first, anxiety set in, I did not become fearful. I knew God had me there for a purpose and all seemed to be quiet around the campgrounds.

I gave my testimony, then Clayton preached and nine people raised their hands who wanted to pray to receive Christ. Our driver, also a church member at Senga Church, asked all those who raised their hands to come kneel at the front. The "front" was about two square feet of floor. People were wall-to-wall, but as we stood, the floor gave way to more space. It was like a picture from *National Geographic* magazine.

Another night Clayton and I had the privilege of meeting Ben Harrye and visiting in his home. He was a kind man who owned 1,500 beef cattle and 400 dairy cattle. He was a Christian and told us he hoped we could convert some of the people living there. The following Sunday he loaned a truck to his people so they could come to be baptized at the Senga Church. Seventeen people piled into the bed of that truck to drive an hour to church. When they arrived they were all smiles, anticipating their baptisms.

My roommate, Brenda Harlow, met a woman in her host church who learned she had AIDS. She told Brenda that she couldn't tell a soul, because they would close down her clothing shop and kick her out of the church. She was raising her three children, plus the four children of her sister who had recently died of AIDS, and she didn't know what would become of the children after she died. Oftentimes children of AIDS victims were left on the doorstep of a pastor.

In spite of my fears of AIDS and the white farmer's plantation situation, I came home unscathed. How thankful I was for prayer partners. I realized more than ever that those at home were truly just as much a part of this trip as I was.

33

Declaring God's Salvation

At supper one night I told the people at my table I couldn't believe I was finally in Africa. As a child I thought most every missionary went to Africa. I remember while working with Girls Auxiliary, a girls' mission organization, we would pray for Zimbabwe, and it seemed to be a place so far away. It's name sounded so African.

"That'll preach!" Clint Henry, one of our team members who was a pastor, commented.

"What do you mean?" I asked.

"It's like God is using you to answer your own prayers," he answered.

It took me a minute to catch on, and then I said, "Wow! That WILL preach!"

All Americans, and sometimes Europeans, in any religious denomination had a night guard. Some even had a day guard. We were restricted from going out at night for any reason unless we were in a group from church. The Peace Corps also had guards.

At church, men and boys sat on one side of the building while women and girls sat on the other side. Although most spoke English, the pastor spoke in Shona, so his sermon was translated into English for our benefit.

Before we arrived, each church member had cards with lines for ten names on each card. The church members prayed for these ten people to receive the Lord at our crusade. When the people who were to participate in visitation were asked to raise their hands, almost everyone's hand went up. Seeing their willingness to serve the Lord was inspired me.

One team member was given a live chicken for leading a woman to Christ. This may seem funny to Americans, but it was a sacrificial gift in Africa.

One afternoon I walked with the women to a college a mile or two from our church. We walked around the campus witnessing to college students. When we approached three young men, two said they were already believers. The third said he wasn't ready to receive Christ.

I told him how God guides us in life and always gives us His best if we follow Him. I told him how we bought our land and how the first two pieces of acreage we had looked at, God closed the door to our purchasing it. Then he gave us some land that we'd never dreamed of, with beautiful oaks, rolling hills, and a couple of ponds.

I also explained that we still have trials and troubles, but we know God is with us. I used my daughter's divorce as an example and told him how God had carried her through it.

Finally, the young man said, "How do you know when you're ready?"

I told him it was like crossing the street. How do you know when to cross it?

When you decide to. I sensed that he expected to "feel something" to determine when he was ready. When he asked if he'd have to give up anything, I told him he might, if God asked him to. He must be willing to do whatever God asked him to do. I explained that God wants the best for us, and it was wonderful to have a father to go to who has all the answers.

Suddenly the young man reached his hand out and said, "Give me that pen!" He filled out the questionnaire and prayed to receive Christ. I couldn't help but praise God right there.

Six men sitting outside between classes also prayed to receive Christ.

One afternoon our helpers were late to meet us at church. While we waited for them, school let out and children were headed in our direction on the way home.

"Here come the kids in blue uniforms," Stacey Ford, a team member said. "They wouldn't let us come to their school, so let's witness to them." So we went out to the road in front of the church to share Jesus with these children. I was reminded of the scripture to go into the highways and hedges and bring them in.

We were batting a thousand. In fact, everyone I witnessed to on my trip received Christ. This was a first for me. Even the two deacons in our church were born again that week. I had heard of the great revival going on in Africa, and now I was witnessing it. Africans were so open and ready to receive the Lord. What a joy it was to work with them and see their fervor to share the love of Christ.

34

The Lion Queen

In mid-week we were scheduled to go on a safari for some R & R. It was a real treat—we saw lions, giraffes, zebras, monkeys, and other animals I had not seen before. What an adventure to see wild animals roaming about. After our safari we were told we would go to the cage of a couple of lion cubs who were eight and ten months old, and we would walk them down to the river and back. The lions, P. K. and Quazy, were each about the size of a large rottweiler with a heavy coat of fur and huge paws.

Mikhail, the cubs' trainer, gave each of us a pole that the cubs respected, and he instructed us that if the cubs got too active, to place the pole in front of us and they would back away. He said they liked to jump at anything hanging down, like camera straps, purses, and coat hems blowing in the wind. We were not to turn our backs on them for a second, because they relished jumping on unsuspecting prey.

I tried to hold my all-weather coat so it wouldn't flap in the continuous breeze. Mikhail warned me a time or two, but what with the wind, it proved to be a difficult task. We walked P. K. and Quazy down to the river, cautiously petting them and taking pictures. They would jump on large rocks and climb up into the trees and do whatever they took a notion to. One lion lay down on a huge rock, so I, not too brave at this point, gently eased up on the rock to have my picture taken with it. On the way back to the cage, the lions continued romping, enjoying their freedom. We moseyed along visiting in small groups and walking at the lions' pace.

The cubs were probably 30 feet away from me, playing in a tree when I turned around to talk to a team member. All of a sudden I felt a thud on my back. I froze, not knowing what to do. The lion's right front paw hit me at the top of my back and its left front paw came down on my left arm. I could feel blood oozing under my four layers of clothing. Standing on its hind legs, the lion cub was as tall as I was.

Everyone screamed, which apparently scared the cub, as it jumped down before I could get scared. The fact that its force did not knock me down remains a puzzle to this day. Everyone wanted to know how I was and if I was okay. I was, but I didn't tell them that I was bleeding.

We walked up on the hill to the cage where Quazy went right in, but P. K. was just having too much fun and didn't want to go in so he stopped at the bottom of the hill and wouldn't go up. Mikhail coaxed and coaxed P. K. to go in, but he just lay there, quite content.

The rest of us had already walked to the top of the hill and watched Mikhail as he worked with the lion cub unsuccessfully.

"Hey, Nancy," someone teased. "Why don't you go down and get that cub to come into its cage." They laughed, while obviously thinking I'd get nowhere near that lion after my frightening episode.

Their challenge was all I needed to spur me on, so I marched down the dusty hill to that stubborn lion cub. I pointed my finger, first at him and then the cage. "You get up from there and go into your cage," I fussed. I looked him square in the eyes. P. K. knew exactly what I meant, and he knew I meant business. He looked at me for a moment, lowered his head and then slowly arose and sauntered up the hill, occasionally looking back as I followed him. I must admit, to have power over a lion proved to be delightfully gratifying. Mikhail thanked me for helping him coax the lion into its cage.

Then Jan Russell, one of our leaders, yelled, "She's the Lion Queen!" The rest of the trip I bore the name "Lion Queen." I told them my ability came because of all the practice I'd had as a school teacher. I only wished my students were so fearful of me.

When we arrived back at village headquarters I took off my jacket, pushed up my sleeves and blood dribbled down my arm. Everyone screamed again, because they hadn't known the lion had punctured my arm in two places. In two days the injury had bruised almost half of my upper arm to a deep purple. Was I a hero or what? And I loved it! My 15 minutes of fame had finally arrived.

The team nurse, Vicki Hickey, concerned about any bacteria I may have received from the puncture, wouldn't let me go out with the group the next day until she contacted the Sanyati Baptist Hospital. A doctor was not available, so Vicki and I waited for a return call. Disappointed I couldn't go out with my team, I decided to go to the hotel beauty shop and massage parlor to witness. Before I went I prayed about how many testimony/questionnaires to take and the Lord spoke, "Four," into my spirit. When I saw four women at the beauty shop and massage parlor I was so excited. The thrill of hearing God never wanes. All four prayed to receive Christ.

A doctor finally called to confirm the antibiotic I was taking for a respiratory infection was sufficient unless the wounds became infected.

After all the hullabaloo died down about the "lion attack," as the team preferred to call it, I remembered Psalm 91 that my prayer warriors were praying over me every day. Wasn't there something in that Psalm about lions? I checked it out, and it reads, "You will trample down lions…"[30] and right before that verse is, "For He orders His angels to protect you wherever you go."[31] *Wow!* I thought. I hadn't been aware of it, but my prayer warriors had been praying that very scripture over me the day the lion jumped on me. I had been covered, spiritually, from the lions and hadn't even realized it. What if my prayer warriors hadn't been praying? What might have happened then? Could the episode have really become a dangerous one? Had the angels protected me from a situation that could have been much worse?

I didn't know all the answers, but one thing I did know. This would be one mission trip I would never forget. I didn't get murdered and had not knowingly met anyone with AIDS, although I don't think having AIDS would have been something people would have broadcasted.

After I was back home in Texas for six months, we were e-mailed the sad news that the pastor's wife of Senga Church had died of AIDS. So I was closer to the deadly disease than I knew. She had taught me how to play the drums, and probably had had AIDS while we were there.

Overcoming fear abroad is not always an easy task, but a promise is a promise, and when God gives it, one can take it to the bank. I came home all in one piece and with one more example of God's faithfulness to add to my memory bank. The one trip that I was most afraid to go on and the one that I had had the most trouble undertaking, turned out to be the best trip of all.

Even though I had a tough start at the beginning of this trip, I knew then that it probably would be a top-notch memorable adventure. I wasn't disappointed.

Proudly showing off my lion wounds.

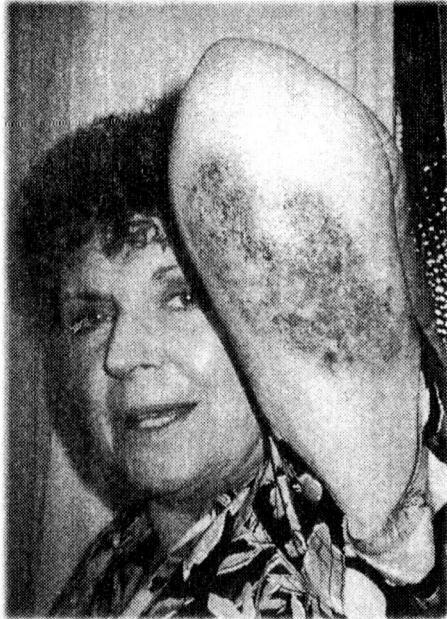

My lion wounds 2 days later.

My 15 minutes of fame as The Lion Queen.

*Dennis Rumbo, Vice President of African Ministries with I. C.,
and me, representing Africa at a missions banquet at
Cornerstone Baptist Church, Terrell, Texas.*

Kenya, 2003

35

Fulfilling a Vision

Having survived a massive cardiac arrest only months after returning from Zimbabwe, I assumed my mission trip days were over. I determined, however, since my mother, grandmother, and great-grandmother had died of heart attacks, that apparently God wasn't finished with me yet, and there was still a purpose for me. Here on earth I loved being a wife, mama, and grandmama, but when summer and mission trip time came around, my heart ached because I couldn't go. I would look at photo albums from previous trips and relive my memories, wishing there was another trip in my future. I was grateful for the 12 trips I had made, but the desire for more was still there.

In January, two years after my heart attack, I signed up for a Dale Carnegie course, because I thought it would be fun. The first class threw me a curve, however, as our homework assignment was to bring back to the class a vision for our lives. I thought, *I can't teach* (I was on disability insurance), *I've fulfilled all my visions, so what kind of vision can I come up with?*

It haunted me, because I didn't have a clue what kind of vision to take back to class. I was happy being a homemaker and doing my church activities, but that about covered my agenda.

My son-in-law, Bob Scott, was a Dale Carnegie instructor, although not mine, so I told him my problem. I definitely needed some help. He studied me for a moment, then said, "Nancy, what is the one thing in the world you would most like to do?"

"Take one more mission trip," I answered, without hesitation.

"Then that's your vision," he replied.

I wanted to laugh, but didn't want to be rude. *You've gotta be kidding,* I thought.

There was no way, physically, that I could go on a mission trip. I didn't think Joe would even consider it, what with my health problems. God had certainly done some glorious repair work on my heart. My physician had said that, in spite of my having had a massive heart attack, there was no heart damage or scar tissue, and my heart looked like new—a God thing. However, I still had high blood pressure, and didn't have the energy to make a trip. I wanted to say to Bob, "That's more of a dream than a vision."

But a seed had been planted.

Although it hadn't, in reality, become my vision yet, I went ahead and used it for my homework. After a few weeks I decided if I exercised regularly and ate right, maybe my body would be in shape to go the following year. So I accepted the dream of another mission trip as a real vision, and hoped that God would give me the faith to see it come to pass.

A couple of months later, on the way to class, the vision was crowding my mind. As I exited off the expressway, the Lord spoke in my spirit that I was to take that mission trip, not next summer, but THIS summer. It was a miracle I didn't have a wreck as I flew around the corner to class. I burst into the room announcing to anyone who would listen that I WAS going on that trip, and I was going THIS summer. I was so excited I couldn't sit still throughout the two-hour class.

I checked out of International Commissions schedule and found there were two trips to Africa planned for summer. It was March by now and I was working hard on my exercise and diet, but progress was much slower than I had anticipated. I knew there was no way I could make the May trip, so it looked like the July trip to Kenya would be my time to go.

Joe knew of my vision, of course, but he had assumed it was for the following summer, so we hadn't discussed the matter much. I had a regular appointment with Dr. Wischmeyer, my cardiologist, that Friday, so I planned to get his approval before telling Joe about the trip. Without my doctor's release, I couldn't go anyway.

I thought Friday would never come, but when it finally did, I took the stress test and then met with Dr. Wischmeyer. I told him of my desire to go to Kenya and eagerly awaited his reply. He looked at me for a moment, and my heart pounded, afraid of what he was about to say, and then he spoke.

"You passed the stress test okay, and since your blood pressure is under control, I see no reason why you shouldn't go to Kenya," Dr. Wischmeyer answered.

I couldn't believe it. His news was too good to be true. I wanted to hug him, but didn't want to embarrass him—or me. Now I could tell Joe about Kenya.

The announcement of an impending mission trip was not immediately usually good news to my husband. While I had already wrestled with the idea of going on a trip and worked through it in prayer before telling Joe, he hadn't had time to deal with the idea yet. So I pretty well knew what his response would be. I met him for lunch after my doctor's appointment and as soon as we sat down I took a deep breath, smiled, and announced, "Honey, I'm going to Kenya THIS July."

He bowed his head and was quiet for a moment. I knew he was concerned for my health. Then he looked up at me and asked, "What does your doctor think of this idea?"

"He released me!" I squealed.

"Well, I need time to think about it," he replied. I understood, and knew he always came around after thinking it over. Had he not, I would not have made any of the trips. I believed strongly in his protective covering over me.

As time passed I became stronger and stronger and was soon walking a mile every day. I felt better than I had since before the heart attack, and I convinced Joe I could handle the trip. I was ready to go— and with his blessing.

Although 150 had signed up for the trip, because of recent terrorist attacks in Kenya, about half the team had canceled, so 82 Africans who had worked on crusades before were to be brought in to help the 76 Americans. I, like those who had already canceled, had to make a decision about whether or not to go. I knew God had called me, and I decided if International Commission canceled the trip, that would certainly be my sign not to go. As destiny would have it, IC did not cancel, so off to Kenya I went.

The first day in Nairobi I went door to door in the church's neighborhood with the pastor of our host church. Because it was a rural area, we walked a long way between houses. He thought nothing of it, but my daily mile ran out long before his legs did. That day turned out to be very discouraging because we didn't catch any fish for Jesus. Most of the homes we visited, people weren't home or were already believers. I told the pastor we needed to go someplace where there were lots of people, like a market.

Wednesday morning I asked the Lord for 20 souls that day. I thought that would be an easy task since we were going to a school. However, when we arrived I learned it was a Christian school, and the teacher told me all the children were already believers. Since the students were from ages 5 to 12, I went ahead with the questionnaire anyway. I assumed that, because of their ages, surely, one of them might not be a believer. All 45 of the children raised their hands to pray to receive Christ, so we prayed the prayer together. Because of what the teacher had told us, however, I did not count any of these children as part of my 20 for the day.

We then went to the market where we prayed with 17 people to receive the Lord. I was disappointed we did not reach my goal of 20, but assumed that maybe three of the school children hadn't really been believers before we arrived.

On the way back to church I asked my helper for the forms people who had prayed to receive the Lord had signed, and much to my surprise when I counted them up, there were 20.

I had miscounted during the day as we were witnessing, and God had given me exactly what I had asked for. With happy tears, I blurted out to our church team, "I asked for 20 souls today, and I have 20 forms!" God had, indeed, answered my prayer.

Throughout our team meeting at the church I continued to weep because I was so grateful for God's faithfulness. The team kept turning to look at me, concerned that something might be wrong. I don't know if I convinced them or not that the tears I was shedding were tears of joy.

Working together in 35 churches we saw 10,114 souls come to the Lord on that trip. Someone asked me before the trip why I wanted to go to Kenya instead of somewhere else. I replied, "Because I may be the only way many will ever hear of Jesus and His love." What an opportunity to share our Lord with people who had no other way to hear about Him. Here in America with our TV's, computers, churches, and daily newspapers, it's hard to believe that the gospel is not readily available to the rest of the world. Yet there are many countries who still have not heard of Jesus.

As we chatted at lunch at church one day our conversation led to pets. Everyone loves to talk about their pets. I asked what they fed their dogs, since I knew people had so little to eat. Our host pastor laughed at my, apparently, absurd question, and he was obviously amazed that in America we waste food on dogs. He replied, "We don't feed dogs. Dogs have to search for their food in trash on the streets." I gathered that's why we saw few dogs on our trip. Cows, pigs and goats also compete with the dogs to find food on city streets. With few "leftovers" from the nationals' meals, finding food proved to be a challenge for the animal kingdom.

In Africa some children are afraid of white people because they are told white people are the "boogey man." Often little kids ran, scared, when they saw us. One little two-year-old girl, Dorees, was petrified of me. She ran behind her mother when I tried to befriend her, and then she'd peek around her mother's skirt at me, with the whites of her eyes shining big as life. She was so beautiful I wanted to bring her home with me. After a couple of days she finally gave me a "high five," and before the end of the week we had become fast friends. She even climbed up into my lap as I taught her to say, "Jesus, Moopy," (what my grandchildren call me), and "So-so (grandmother) Nancy." She was so proud of herself when she would repeat my words. When she did, I'd hug her and brag on her, which was something you didn't often see in African culture. Hugging and loving on one's child was not a practice there, which might have been the reason Dorees and I became such great friends. I think she thoroughly enjoyed my hugging and loving on her.

The church kids loved the Wal-mart smiley stickers that we'd stick on their foreheads. One day after I had stuck one on Dorees' head and then on a few others, Dorees nudged up to me and pointed to her cheeks. We usually limited our stickers to one per kid so we'd have enough to last all week, but I couldn't resist this little one, so I stuck one on each of her cheeks, too. Then I grabbed my camera and took her picture, my favorite picture from the whole trip. When we left church the last day, Dorees cried and cried because she wanted to go with me. And I shed a few tears myself. How quickly we bond to these precious ones in such a short time. I'll never forget her.

Because I was physically able to work only half of each day, I suspected this would be my last mission trip. The walking didn't tire me as much as the constant talking for several straight hours. I told my family about it the night that I returned home, but because I was always homesick and weary before returning home from my trips, they laughed and said, "Oh, Mom, you always feel that way when you come home." This time, however, I meant it. I believed I had returned from my last mission trip.

In church the following Sunday, the Lord spoke to Cyndi, our oldest daughter, that He was passing my mantle on to her. I didn't even know I had a mantle. She was so touched she shared God's message with her church. Three months later she and her husband, Bob, went on their first mission trip to Peru.

Cyndi's word from God confirmed to me that my era of mission trips had come to an end. I'm grateful to God for allowing me 13 mission trips in 20 countries on five continents. As a teenager I had no idea how my favorite scripture, Proverbs 3:5-6, would impact my life. It reads, "Trust in the Lord with all thine heart; and lean not unto thine own understanding. In all thy ways, acknowledge Him, and *He shall direct thy paths*."[32]

Perhaps, one of the best lessons I've learned from my mission trips is if you are willing to live life God's way, He'll take you places and give you experiences that you never even dreamed of. His dreams for us are always bigger than our own.

"God can do anything—far more than you could ever imagine or request in your wildest dreams! He does it not by pushing us around but by working within us, his Spirit deeply and gently within us." [33]

He really does give the best to those who leave the choice with Him. Who knows? He may even lead you to become a suitcase carrier for God someday.

Conclusion

Thankful for Traffic, Commodes and Home

When I was away from home on the mission field, blessings once taken for granted became of monumental importance.

From my journal I wrote:

"I AM THANKFUL FOR AMERICAN 5:00 TRAFFIC. If you haven't ridden in a taxi in Bogota, Columbia, you're in for one hair-raising adventure. The main streets afford traffic lights but not the side streets. We're talking downtown here.

"Their method is that whoever arrives at the intersection first, honks, thereby warning other drivers he has the right-of-way. We're not talking about slowing down at the intersection either. As we drove, horrified, I opened my Bible to Psalm 91, and reminded God of His promise to protect us. I was hanging on to His promise for my life. I realized that as bad as our Texas 5 o'clock traffic might be, it would be a welcomed venture compared to driving in Bogota.

* * *

"I'M THANKFUL FOR CHICKEN, THE AMERICAN WAY. Before my trip to Peru I discovered a scripture that was difficult to swallow. No pun intended. It reads that before one ministers to people, he must first eat the food they set before him by the nationals.

Considering food I'd eaten in other countries, my first thought was, *You've got to be kidding!* But there it was. I wondered if this scripture was some kind of forewarning.

"In Peru the gracious hostess sat before me a bowl of vegetable soup. Looking up at me, floating in the midst of the veggies was a yellow, wrinkled chicken's foot, no doubt the chef's touch of perfection in Peru. I stared at it in wonder, and then I remembered the recently learned scripture. *What do I do with that?* I wondered.

"I choked as I ate all around the chicken foot. I remembered my grandparents' farm and how the chickens ran loose all over the place. I also remembered what I stepped in at the farm when I ran barefooted all over the place, and that the chicks stepped in it, too. And I was supposed to eat this? After I had eaten the potatoes, corn, onions and broth, the foot lay in the bottom of the bowl, daring me. 'Oh, God, I just can't do it. Please, forgive me,' I sadly prayed.

* * *

"At an elite hotel in Canton, China, we were served a seven-course meal. I picked at it as Chinese food, the China way, was not my cup of tea. What I would've given for a good old McDonald's hamburger.

"We heard we were going to be served chicken, one of my favorites. *Great!* I thought. *Something American, finally!* What could they possibly do wrong to chicken? I soon found out.

"The chicken, head and all, arrived on a fancy platter, sliced like one would slice a roast, bone and all. My desire for chicken left me.

* * *

"I'M THANKFUL FOR COMMODES, AMERICAN STYLE. In Moscow as we waited at the airport for our luggage to come around on the belt, we decided it was restroom break time. As we neared the ladies' room, the stench stopped us in our tracks. Due to necessity we chose to continue on, discovering the 'commode' was nothing but a hole in the floor over which one stood.

"We later learned that the employees at the airport received pay whether they worked or not, so those assigned to the bathrooms preferred not to work. That's socialism for you. However, I couldn't blame them.

* * *

"At our exclusive hotel in Kiev, in the Ukraine, we were relieved to find American-type commodes in our rooms, only to learn that none of the 200 in the entire hotel worked properly.

"The hotel housekeeper told us that new commodes and parts had been on order for two years. I halfway repaired ours with a rubber band so, it would, at least, flush. But the water in the tank continued to run, and it overflowed about every other day.

* * *

"I'M THANKFUL FOR AVAILABLE MEDICINE. In Moscow I invited Emma, a tour guide from my former trip, to our hotel to give her clothes, food and other items we had brought for her new baby. When one of the team members offered her baby aspirin, over-the-counter cold and cough medicine and vitamins, Emma asked if he was a doctor. It amazed her that anyone could freely purchase such items over the counter.

* * *

"I'M THANKFUL FOR THE FREEDOM TO OWN A BIBLE, AMERICA'S BEAUTIFUL CHURCHES, AND THE FREEDOM TO WORSHIP. When the Communists took over in China, all church steeples, crosses, and stained glass windows were destroyed. Bibles were outlawed so smuggled-in Bibles were torn apart in sections and passed around for families to read. Sometimes a family might receive only a page. That is still the case today.

"When we visited the 'Attic Church,' nationals packed the first two floors to watch our service in the attic by closed-circuit television. According to Nora Lam, the pastor, Lin Xiangao, was the most loved and famous underground church leader in all of China. He believed it was his duty to suffer for God and had spent more than 20 years as a slave laborer in a communist coal mine and prisons.

* * *

"After meeting and talking with a young Nigerian immigrant, Charity Abaraoha, at a women's church retreat in Dallas, I asked what was the one thing she liked best about America. She thought for a moment, and then replied, 'The freedom of speech. If we speak out in certain parts of Nigeria about Christianity or our political leaders, the lives of our family members will be in danger.'

* * *

"I'M THANKFUL FOR MY HOME. As we walked the neighborhoods in Brazil, sharing the good news of Jesus, to my surprise I found the homes had dirt floors. A table was usually the only furniture in the one room house. There were mats to sit on which doubled as beds at night.

"In Africa the huts, probably 10 to 15 feet in diameter, were made of slender tree trunks tied together to form a circle, and covered with thatch roofs. Straw mats provided the only 'furniture' with a fire in the middle of the hut.

"Back at home after a mission trip, as I drove over the cattle guard to see granddaddy oaks, our lake, my beautiful collie, Joe's lovable boxer, and our lovely two-story yellow house with flowers all around, I marveled that God would allow me to be born in America. I was reminded that to whom much is given, much is required. The best part about a trip was coming home, and I would never again take America for granted."

Testimony/Questionnaire

THE TESTIMONY/QUESTIONNAIRE USED IN WITNESSING INTERNATIONAL COMMISSION, INC. (INDIVIDUALIZED FOR EACH TEAM MEMBER)

Hello. My name is Nancy Cobb, and I am a believer in Jesus Christ. My husband and I have 3 lovely daughters who have borne us 10 wonderful grandchildren. My husband serves as a deacon in our church, where I work along with him. I also am a former English teacher of 5th grade students, and I enjoy gardening, playing the piano, and loving on my grandchildren.

From the time I was born, I was told Jesus loved me by my parents, and especially by my grandmother. My grandmother would tell us "the Jesus story" each Sunday morning as we drove out to our little country church, and I would cry when she told us about Jesus dying on the cross for my sins. At age 11 I asked Jesus to forgive me of my sins and come into my heart, which He did. Throughout my teen years I followed Him and hungered after His Word. I served Him, read my Bible daily, and prayed, but I didn't know Him in an intimate way, just like one person knows another, until much later.

It was not until my 30s that I began to have a one on one relationship with Him, and He began to teach me much in His Word. Although I had read the Bible all of my life, I began to read it like a love letter from my Lord, written especially to me. It came alive, and I began to learn what faith was all about, that it was simply trusting God in every area of my life. I recognized that He was in control of my life and would work all things out for my good if I would trust Him. Life became exciting as I saw God working in my life each day. I felt like I was in a big bubble of love.

My favorite scripture is, "Trust in the Lord with all your heart, and don't lean on your own understanding. In all your ways acknowledge Him, and He will direct your paths." Proverbs 3:5-6. By trusting Him, He has, indeed, directed my path to YOU this very day.

I picked up a heavy suitcase in my middle-school years and damaged my spinal cord, which gave me great pain off and on for over 30 years. The pain got so bad that I thought I would not be able to stand up in the choir much longer at church. Then one morning at a prayer meeting about 20 years ago, God reached down and touched my back. I was totally healed, which my doctor confirmed with x-rays, and now I've walked many miles since then on mission trips all over the world. I have become a suitcase carrier for God.

God has also worked miracles, financially, that I might make these trips. Where He guides, He provides, and once a stranger paid my way to Russia. I know that when He calls me on a trip, He will, somehow, supply my need. He always has. I'm in your country today, because many friends and family paid my way that I might come to tell you of my wonderful Jesus. He loves you and me more than we could ever imagine, and I came all the way from America just to tell you that.

GOD'S PLAN FOR YOUR SALVATION

1. Do you believe in God?   Yes_____ No_____
2. Do you believe that God loves you?   Yes_____ No_____
3. Do you believe that Jesus Christ is the Son of God? (John 20:31)   Yes_____ No_____
4. Do you believe that you are a sinner? (Romans 3:23)   Yes_____ No_____
5. Do you believe that Jesus Christ died for your sins? (Romans 5:8)   Yes_____ No_____
6. Do you want Jesus Christ to save you from your sins?(Romans 6:23)   Yes_____ No_____
7. Jesus said, "*I am the way, the truth, and the life: no man comes unto the Father, but by Me.*" (John 14:6)
   The Bible says: "*That if you shall confess with your mouth the Lord Jesus Christ and shall believe in your heart that God raised Him from the dead, you shall be saved.*"
   The Scripture says: "*For whosoever shall call upon the name of the Lord shall be saved.*" (Romans 10:9-13)
   Do you believe this?   Yes_____ No_____
8. Jesus Christ is God's only Son. Are you willing to call upon Him so your sins will be forgiven?   Yes_____ No_____

(continued)

SUITCASE CARRIER FOR GOD

An Example of Prayer

Dear Lord, I know I have done wrong and need forgiveness. Thank you for dying for my sins and for offering me eternal life. Please, forgive me of my sins and help me turn from them. I now confess you as my Savior. Take control of my life and help me live for Jesus. Thank you for coming into my life and giving me eternal life. In Jesus' name I pray. Amen.

You can receive Christ into your heart if you repent and trust in Him as expressed in the prayer.

9. Will you now pray this prayer in
   your own words?   Yes_____ No_____
10. Now that you have prayed, do you
    believe that Jesus Christ has forgiven
    you and saved you from your sins?
    (John 1:12)   Yes_____ No_____

"How shall they preach unless they are **sent**?" Romans 10:15
Many, many thanks to each of my partners who contributed to **send** the gospel around the world. Without your participation, these trips would not have been made possible.

(Deceased=dec.)

Adair, John (dec.) & Jan
Adams, Dave
Anderson, Mark & Terri
Arnette, Lucille (dec.)
Armstrong, Deweene
Baker, Norman & Jean
Barnes, Charles & Nelda
Beacham, Melva Lea
Benninger, DeeDee
Brewer, Royce & Laxie
Brown, Bob
Brown, Ron & Betty
Burnett, Mark & Janine
Burris, George & June
Burton, Rev. Charles & Sharon
Campbell, William (dec.) & Becky (dec.)
Carlson, Roger & Faye
Caswell, Don & Teri
Casa View Baptist Church, Dallas, TX
Cline, Glen (dec.) & Mary Rene
Cobb, Frankie (dec.)
Cobb, Joe
Cobb, Jesse & Lynda
Cobb, Dr. Jimmy & Sue
Cobb, Nan (dec.)
Colacecchi, Scott & Cindy
Conrad, Cheryl
Conrad, Dr. Curt & Cami, Cristen, Cassie & Cathleen

Cooper, Emma (dec.)
Cooper, Rev. Ken & Charlet Cooper
Cornerstone Baptist Church, Terrell, TX
Crow, Richard & Judy
Cummings, Norman & Alva Jean
Dance, Juanita (dec.)
Dance, Kenny & Bobbie Carole
Denton, Curt & Tina
Denton, Loyd & Leslie
Dimsdle, Royce & Dona
Downing, Sam (dec.) & Jackie
Duffey, John (dec.) & Sue
Dunham, Mike & Cindi
Ellis, Drs. Bob & Luanne
Evans, Max & Geraldine
Ferguson, Don & Dr. Caren
Foster, Mary Nan
Frank, Karl
Frank, Mary
Free, Don (dec.)
Freeman, Bill & Deryl
Freeman, Frank & Freda
Gibbs, Justin
Glover, Kay
Guritz, Elmer & Carol
Guynes, Jean
Hall, Euda Mae (dec.)
Hamilton, Clyde
Hamilton, Emma (dec.)
Hamontree, Mike & Arlene
Hamontree Sunday School Class, Casa View Baptist Church, Dallas, TX
Heasley, Sam & Jacque
Hetmer, Al & Gloria
Heuer, Martha
Heyland, Gary & Maryann

Hogan, Duane & Pamela
Holleman, Allen & Sandy
Hooker, Dr. J. Bennett (dec.) & Ione
Hull, Karen
Jobe, Dan & Martha
Jobe, Rev. Mark & Sandy
Johnson, Elsie (dec.)
Johnston, Jana
Jones, Rev. Larry & Joy
Kilcrease, George & Marie
Kines, Jerry & Margaret
Kirkland, Mary Ann
Knox, Jimmie & Ann
Kopecky, Peggy
Lawler, Suzi
Lea, Dr. Larry
Lord, Curtis
Markham, Eva Jo
Martin, Wanda
Mathews, John & Maellen
McCary, Glenn
McGinnis, Bertha
McHone, Gene & Dixie
Milliman, Byron & Betty
Mitchell, Jack & Reva
Mitchell, Misti Page
Morgan, Doug & Lynn
Morgan, Rick & Lauree
Morris, Karl & Susan
Mosser, Mark & Michele
Murphy, Dick & Linda
Nix, Mike
Noakes, Addilu
Opel, Felecia
Page, Rev. Don (dec.) & Marie

Page, Gary & Cathi, Crystal, Preston & Parker
Palmer, Ray & Janet
Peavy, Glenn & Lou
Peters, Pete & Pat
Petrea, Terry & Terri
Phillips, Ed
Ponder, Rev. Lowell (dec.)
Pope, Del & Nancy
Pou, Bill (dec.) & Julia
Powell, Jimmy & Patsy
Price, Dr. Bob & Janett
Ratliff, Jack (dec.) & Jan
Restoration Worship Center, Plano, TX
Roberts, Willis (dec.) and Millie (dec.)
Robinson, Ann
Rodgers, Shafner (dec.) &Ruth (dec.)
Rogers, Rev. Russell & Shelley
Rumbo, Dennis
Rumbo, Mona
Sanders, Lane & Debra
Scott, Bob & Cyndi, Don, Joel & Seth Sartain
Seay, Jimmy & Cindy
Self, Gale & Saundra
Shaffer, Hubert & Ethel
Shibley, Dr. David & Naomi
Small, Johnny & Ann
Smith, Doug & Robyn
Snyder, Robert & Sue
Stockman, Perry
Thurman, L. Don & LaDonna
Todd, Leonard
Welch, Noble & Pat
Wells, Gerald & Bettye
White, Bill & Vernell
Whitt, Mary (dec.)

Wilson, Effie C.
Wilson, Hazel (dec.)
Wilson, Hugh (dec.) & Sibyl (dec.)
Wilson, Max
Wilson, Wysondria
Wreyford, Norman, Sr. (dec.) & Dorothy
Wreyford, Norman, Jr. (dec.) & Tammy
Wuethrich, Tom

If your name has been inadvertently omitted, please forgive me. Just remember, God knows!

End Notes

[1] Holy Bible, New Living Translation, Psalm 96:3, Tyndale House Publishers, Inc., Wheaton, IL, p 627

[2] Holy Bible, New Living Translation, Psalm 78:4, 6, 7, Tyndale House Publishers, Inc., Wheaton, IL, p 613

[3] What a Friend We Have in Jesus (song title), Joseph Scriven, 1855; Charles C. Converse, 1868

[4] New American Standard Bible, Isaiah 52:7, The Lockman Foundation, La Habra, CA, 1973, p 1029

[5] The Good News Translation in Today's English Version, (GNT), Psalm 16:1, 5B, 9-11, American Bible Society, 1976, pp 601-02

[6] New American Standard Bible, New Testament, John 20:21, 22, The Lockman Foundation, La Habra, CA, 1973, p 177

[7] New American Standard Bible, New Testament, Acts 3:6, The Lockman Foundation, La Habra, CA, 1973, p 184

[8] The Amplified Bible, New Testament, Philippians 4:19, The Lockman Foundation, Las Habra, CA, 1965, p 310

[9] Holy Bible, New Living Translation, Psalm 37:4, Tyndale House Publishers, Inc., Wheaton, IL, 1996, p 586

[10] Holy Bible, New Living Translation, Luke 9:1, Tyndale House Publishers, Inc., Wheaton IL, 1996, p 1038

[11] Holy Bible, New Living Translation, Luke 10:20, Tyndale House Publishers, Inc., Wheaton, IL, 1996, p 1041

[12] New American Standard Bible, New Testament, Matthew 7:7, The Lockman Foundation, La Habra, CA, 1973, p9

[13] Holy Bible, New Living Translation, Psalm 121:1, 2, Tyndale House Publishers, Inc. Wheaton, IL, p 648

[14] The Amplified Bible, Old Testament, Exodus 9:16, The Lockman Foundation, 1965, p 79

[15] Holy Bible, Contemporary English Version, Acts 3:6-10, American Bible Society, New York, 1995, p 255

[16] Holy Bible, New Living Translation, Isaiah 55:8, 9, Tyndale House Publishers, Inc., Wheaton, IL, p 745

[17] When the Roll is Called up Yonder (song title), James M. Black, 1893, public domain

[18] New American Standard Bible, Psalm 37:4, The Lockman Foundation, La Habra, CA, 1973, p 792

[19] New American Standard Bible, Psalm 91:10b, The Lockman Foundation, La Habra, CA, 1973, p 846

[20] The Good News Translation in Today's English Version, Psalm 41:2b, 3, American Bible Society, 1976, p 620

[21] New Living Translation, Holy Bible, Psalm 138:8, Tyndale House Publishers, Inc., Wheaton, IL, p 653

[22] New Living Translation, Holy Bible, Psalm 139:3a, Tyndale House Publishers, Inc., Wheaton, IL 1996, p 653

[23] New American Standard Bible, New Testament, I Thess. 5:17, The Lockman Foundation, La Habra, CA, 1973, p 316

[24] New American Standard Bible, Old Testament, Isaiah 55:8b, The Lockman Foundation, La Habra, CA, 1973, p 1033

[25] The Good News Translation in Today's English Version, Psalm 41:3, American Bible Society, 1976, p 620

[26] New Living Translation, Holy Bible, John 14:6, Tyndale House Publishers, Inc., Wheaton, IL, 1996, p 1085

[27] Holy Bible, New Living Translation, Acts 4:18-20, Tyndale House Publishers, Inc., Wheaton, IL, 1996, p 1099

[28] Holy Bible, New Living Translation, Psalm 91:7, Tyndale House Publishers, Inc., Wheaton, IL, 1996, p 624

[29] You Are in Control (song title), Scott Underwood, Mercy/Vineyard Publishing (ASCAP), 1997

[30] Holy Bible, New Living Translation, Psalm 91:13, Tyndale Publishers, Inc., Wheaton, IL, 1996, p 624

[31] Holy Bible, New Living Translation, Psalm 91:11, Tyndale Publishers, Inc., Wheaton, IL, 1996, p 624

[32] The Holy Bible, Authorized King James Version, Proverbs 3:5-6, Harpers and Brothers Publishers, New York, p 610

[33] The Message, Ephesians 3:20, NavPress, Colorado Springs, Colorado, 2002, p 2129